Praise for How to M
Agent

"I just received my real estate license, and .... has opened my eyes concerning all the things I can do with said license. As I was going through the process of obtaining my license, I only thought about helping people buy and sell houses, but after reading this book I realize there is so much more I can do! Thank you, Mark!"
-Sharonda Bethel

"I would definitely recommend this book to anyone considering a job in real estate. Considering the loads of valuable content within the hundreds of insightful pages, this book is practically a steal for the price. This is by far Mark's best piece of writing. I have read many of his previous self-published books, and this one stands out from the rest. He has really improved as a writer since his very first one."
-William Spencer

"I have utilized the articles and podcasts available on investfourmore.com for the past year or so, and it has really helped me grow and change my mindset as an investor. I decided to obtain my real estate license a few months ago and bought this book to gather some ideas to help me get started. It is a great resource, and I would recommend it to anyone with their license or thinking about getting their license!"
-J Bohler

"Mark's books have been awesome! I started out on this one as a new agent and found his advice to be very practical and something you could actually do. I am looking at his coaching and some of his other books to propel myself forward in my new career as a real estate agent / investor."
-Steve Portock

"Top notch information!! Do yourself a favor and follow Mark Ferguson's blog and podcasts for access to his GAME

CHANGING wealth of knowledge! I have personally used his experiences and information first-hand and have already seen results! THANKS MARK!"

-Patrick Roob

"There are many great suggestions in How to Make It Big As A Real Estate Agent. I am returning to real estate sales after a several decades long hiatus and have a game plan to implement which lines up with those which Mark has used. But the idea of building a team is a new one to me and is one I will implement. Great advice for new agents, particularly making it clear the extent of dedication and hard work required to achieve the upper levels of success. I strongly recommend this book."

-Ray Lang

"Perfect information, should be standard reading for agents."

-Trevor McDaniels

How to Make it Big as a Real Estate Agent

The right systems and approaches to cut years off your learning curve and become successful in real estate.

From Real Estate Expert
Mark Ferguson

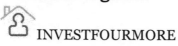 INVESTFOURMORE

ISBN-10: 153366160X
ISBN-13: 978-1533661609

Cover Design: Pixel Studio
Interior Design: Justin Gesso
Editing: Gregory Alan Helmerick
Printed in the USA

Table of Contents

Special Bonus and Agent Tools

This book is packed with usable, realistic, and proven techniques anyone can use to become a successful real estate agent, Realtor, or broker.

Keeping yourself accountable and utilizing all the techniques I cover in this book can be difficult. First off, don't stress if you don't do everything I cover! The fact that you can't do everything at once is a good things! Too many agents try 8,000 different marketing techniques and fail miserably. In real estate, focus is key and doing a few things really well will always be better than doing 100 things mediocrely.

If you only learn one thing upon first reading this book, it will help you. The next time you read it, maybe you'll implement a few other things and start slowly building a solid foundation for success. If you take your time mastering one thing at a time, you will be much more successful than if you do 10 things halfway at once.

It may help to take notes while you read or to pause frequently on the things that really hit home with you or you feel will help you the most.

While this book contains everything you need to be successful, some people want a little more help. If you think you need more coaching or someone to bounce ideas off, I offer coaching programs and a wonderful blog with many free resources. You can find the blog and special discounts on my coaching at the link below.

https://investfourmore.com/bonus

How to Use this Book

I wrote this for anyone who is, wants to become, or has thought about being an agent at any point in their life. There is a lot of misinformation about real estate agents, including how much money they make, how hard it is, what the day-to-day activities are like, and how much you must work. I have been a licensed Realtor since 2001, and in this book, I present the reality of being an agent. Being a great agent doesn't take rocket science; it isn't even difficult. It does take focus, a plan, dedication, and perseverance. If you know what to do and what to expect before you become an agent, success will come much quicker than if you try to figure it all out on your own.

I have a team of ten, six of which are licensed agents, and they handle almost all the transactions on our team. The great part about real estate is you can create a business that mostly runs itself. At one point in my career, I was selling 200 houses on my own every year. However, that was a very stressful time in my life, and I much prefer having others doing most of the work while I concentrate on making my business better. I cover all of this later in the book and show you how to create a sustainable and valuable real estate business, not just how to sell houses.

Thanks to real estate, I have been able to provide an awesome life for me and my family. As an agent, not only have I sold many houses, but I have also invested heavily in real estate. None of that would have been possible if I didn't get my real estate license and learn the business from an agent's perspective.

Below are a few of my career highlights (I am 37 now). This may sound like bragging, but I am proud of what I have accomplished, and being a successful agent greatly contributed to my success.

- I own 16 rentals that earn me about $8,000 per month. I bought each rental with 20 or 25 percent down. I bought each one at 25 percent or more below market value.

- I invested about $300,000 to buy and renovate them, and they now have over $1.6 million in equity. I started buying rentals in 2010, so that is a pretty decent return.
- I have been a Realtor for 15 years and run a real estate sales team of 10. They sell from 100 to 200 houses per year
- I also flip 10 to 15 houses per year. In 2017, I have around 16 flips going at once and average about a $30,000 profit on each flip I complete.
- I started InvestFourMore.com in 2013, and it has since become one of the most popular real estate blogs around, with over 300,000 views per month.
- I have been featured on the Washington Post, MSN, Yahoo, Zilllow, Realtor.com, The Street, Forbes, The Huffington Post, and many other large media outlets.

If you like this book, please let me know. Send an email to Mark@investfourmore.com. I personally respond to all emails and love hearing from my readers. Please leave me a review on Amazon as well.

Introduction

I did not plan on a career in real estate, but it has been very good to me. In 2001, I graduated from the University of Colorado with a degree in Business Finance. I looked for jobs in the banking industry because I liked money, and I wanted to make a lot of it. My job search wasn't successful, so I decided to move back home and help my dad with his real estate business...temporarily. I helped with selling houses and with his fix and flips. I liked the flexibility being an agent afforded, and I also loved working on the flips. After a few months, I decided to get my real estate license and try being an agent myself. It was not always easy, but I am sure glad I did it. I found some early success, but when I finally found my niche and specialty, things took off. I was selling hundreds of houses per year, buying rentals, flipping houses, and even creating my blog. I am really happy I did not find a decent banking job!

At the beginning of my real estate career, I struggled to make money and find a niche. But one of the great things about real estate is the multiple options available for making money. I am a natural introvert, and marketing myself to clients and getting business wasn't easy. Once I learned to diversify into areas of real estate that fit me, my career took off. I found the world of REO and loved it from the beginning. REO has made me a lot of money, but this book is not all about REO. There are many different ways to make money in real estate and many different areas of expertise that require different skills. REO helped me create a team and learn how to sell houses in multiple ways and in multiple markets. In 2017, REO is virtually non-existent in Colorado, but I am still making a ton of money with my real estate team. The best part is, I don't do most of the work! My team does most of the selling, and I am free to pursue my investing, the blog, or just hanging out with my family. That is the great part about real estate. You can set it up to be a business, and with the right people, it can run by itself. In the beginning, you can make a lot of money as an agent, despite what the stats say.

Starting out in real estate can be very challenging, especially if you do not have the support of a mentor to guide you. In this book, I will explain the different ways you can make money, how much money you can make, how hard it is to become an agent, and what you need to do once you become a successful agent. As a bonus, I will show you how to create a team and hire people to propel you even further.

If you've ever wanted to invest in real estate, I discuss how being an agent will make that easier and earn you more money.

PART I

CHAPTER 1

How Do Real Estate Agents Make Money?

Many people think of real estate agents as chauffeurs. Agents drive prospective buyers around town, show them houses for sale, and hopefully after a few weeks of searching, the buyers decide on a house. Driving buyers around can be part of the real estate business, but there are many other ways for agents to make money. I have not had a buyer in my car for years, and even when I worked with a lot of buyers, I rarely drove them anywhere. Most buyers have a car and are perfectly capable of driving it to different houses. Don't think that being a chauffeur and an agent are the same thing. When agents become super successful, they realize how valuable their time is. As their career develops, many agents start their own team or work strictly with listings. One of the great things about being an agent is you can turn it into a business that offers multiple ways to make a living.

How do agents get paid?

Most agents work on commission. They only get paid when they sell a house. If you happen to be one of those agents who drives buyers around all day, and those buyers never buy a house, you are working for free. In reality, you are actually paying to work due to the gas you are wasting. People think that agents make a ton of money because the commissions on a completed sale can be high. But people do not realize how much time agents spend on marketing, prospecting, training, and driving buyers around. Do not let these things scare you off! Yes, you can spend a lot of time on tasks without getting a pay check, but if you become a great agent, you can make an awesome living.

How much do agents make?

The average (or median) income for agents can be surprisingly low. Usually, the average agent's income ranges from $30,000 to $50,000, depending on which source you use. A lot of potential agents give up when they see most make only $40,000. You must remember that those statistics include agents who only work part time, and most agents do not know how to make money. Three agents in our office consistently make over $300,000 per year from sales alone, and I am in a town with 100,000 people and relatively low house prices. Many agents across the country make over $1 million annually.

Most full-time agents make much more than $40,000 per year. There are over 1 million agents in the United States, and income statistics can be very misleading because many agents only work part time. I could not find data showing how many part-time versus full-time agents exist, but those part-time agents bring the median income down. There is also a difference between Realtors and real estate agents, which I will talk more about later. Realtors who work 40 hours per week average $54,000 annually, and Realtors who work over 60 hours per week average over $87,000. You do not have to work 60 or more hours per week to make that much. You just have to work smarter.

Not only do part-time agents bring that income down, but I believe there many agents that simply don't work hard. In real estate, you are your own boss, and you must push yourself to succeed. To be honest, many people think being an agent is a free ride and easy money. Buyers constantly tell me they must call three or four agents before one will answer their phone or call them back. I recently tried to send a referral to an agent in Florida, and I had to contact five agents before one responded! If all agents worked hard, buyers would never need to call multiple agents to get a return call.

What are the different ways real estate agents can make money?

Working with buyers

The most common way for an agent to make money is as a buyer's agent. A buyer's agent works primarily with people looking to buy a house. The agent will look up houses for sale, show houses, write offers on houses for buyers, and help the buyers throughout the transaction. Buyer's agents will also work with sellers, but mostly when the buyer needs to sell their house in order to buy a new one.

Buyer's agents can make good money, but working with buyers takes a lot of time. For each buyer, you must find and show houses and write offers before the escrow process starts. Some buyers will want to see many houses and others only a few. Buyers are understandably picky, and helping buyers find a house they love can take hours. I recently worked with some friends who were looking for a house, and they only viewed one before writing an offer. On the other hand, Nikki—one of the agents on my team—recently worked with buyers who looked at over 50 houses before writing an offer.

Here are some other tasks that the buyer's agent helps with:

- **Getting a buyer approved for financing:** You do not want to work with a buyer who is not approved—or at least qualified—to buy a house. Agents will communicate with the lender and the buyer to make sure everyone is on the same page.
- **Writing contracts:** Agents write contracts for buyers, which is not as complicated as it sounds. Most states have approved contracts, and agents fill in the blanks. They do not write contracts from scratch. Agents also help the buyers negotiate with the seller.
- **Finding an inspector:** Most buyers will want to complete an inspection, and their agent may provide a few names for the buyer to choose from. The agent can also help the buyer decide if they should ask the sellers

to make repairs or other concessions based on the inspection.

- **Finding houses for sale**: Agents are usually responsible for checking the MLS (multiple listing service) and sending the buyers a list of houses for sale.
- **Dealing with appraisals:** In some cases, an appraisal may come in low or uncover required repairs. The agent is responsible for helping the buyer work through appraisals.
- **Coordinating closings:** When a house sells, it is usually called a closing. Agents work with attorneys or title companies to coordinate when and where the closing will be.
- **Dealing with different types of sellers:** Some sellers, like HUD (government owned foreclosures) and REO, (bank foreclosures) have very different processes for submitting offers, inspections, appraisals and more. A buyer's agent needs to make sure they are educated and know how to deal with different types of sellers. For example, HUD does not pay for title insurance, which most sellers customarily do.

How much money does a buyer's agent make?

A buyer's agent earns commissions on each sale. There is no set or typical commission, but I will use a 3-percent commission as an example (which is what HUD pays buyer's agents). The buyer's agent may not get to keep all their commission because, in most cases, they must pay their broker a split. We will assume the split is 70 percent to the agent and 30 percent to the broker (I talk more about splits later in the book). If an agent works hard—and works full time—they can sell 20 houses per year...no problem. In my market, the average house price is $175,000, so a real estate agent could earn over $70,000 in this scenario ($175,000 x 20 houses x .03 commission x .7 split to the broker equals $73,500).

Agents must consider expenses like office bills, MLS fees, insurance, and other miscellaneous items. Those fees will vary depending on the agent's agreement with their broker. Total expenses should be under $5,000 per year depending on the office setup. If an agent sells more than 20 houses per year, which is very possible, yearly income can rise significantly. Usually, the more houses an agent sells, the smaller the broker split will be. Even if you don't work as hard or have a tough time and sell less than 20 houses, you can make a living. A buyer's agent may also sell listings for sellers who they are helping to buy a house. A buyer's agent is not limited to only selling to buyers, but that is their focus. The biggest issue with being a buyer's agent is their income is limited to how much time they have in the day.

Working with sellers

Many agents also make money by listing houses for sellers. Listing simply means putting the house up for sale. Many agents strive to be listing agents because it takes less time to list a house than it does to sell one. Working listings doesn't require driving buyers around. When agents list a house for sellers, they also have the potential to attract buyers. The more listings an agent has, the more buyer leads they will bring in. If you can work with both the buyer and seller of a house, you can make twice as much money because you get two commissions instead of one. Working with multiple sellers allows an agent to start a team because they can hire agents who will work with buyers. Later, I'll discuss using teams. That is how I love to run my business because I make money from my agents without doing much work.

Here are many of the tasks associated with listing a house:

- **Determining market value:** One of the most important parts of selling a house is listing it at the right price. List too high and the seller will lose money; list too low and they will lose money.
- **Determining what to repair:** The better condition a house is in when sold, the more money the seller will usually make. Some sellers will not be able to make repairs, and some repairs are more valuable than others. An agent can help the seller determine what to repair and what not to repair.

- **Informing the seller of associated costs:** An agent should give a net sheet to the seller so they know what the agent charges, what the title and closing fees will be, what the taxes will be, and what any other costs will be so there are no surprises at closing.
- **Listing the house in the MLS:** An agent will take pictures of the house, take measurements, and list all the features of the house. Agents will take that information and list it in the MLS system so other agents can find the listing and show it to their buyers.
- **Negotiating with buyers:** Agents will help the seller negotiate all the terms of the contract, like the price, inspections, inclusions, and more.
- **Coordinating closings:** Agents will help the seller choose a title company or attorney and set up the closing.

Working with corporate sellers

Some sellers are just regular people looking to sell their house, and some sellers are corporate. The government, banks, relocation companies, builders, and investment companies all sell houses and need real estate agents. Some corporate sellers, if big enough, will have their own sales department, and others will use local agents. If you can become a listing agent for a builder, a relocation company, the government, or a bank, you may find a steady stream of listings coming your way week after week. With those listings come more buyer leads and the opportunity to start a team.

For an agent who is just getting started, working for a large corporate seller who has hundreds of listings is not realistic. Getting in with these sellers takes time and experience. I am a HUD and REO listing agent, and it took me years to build my business to where it is today. However, when the country was at the peak of the foreclosure market, I was selling over 200 houses per year. Working with some type of company, builder, or investor who has a lot of listings should be part of every agent's goals and plans.

How much money can an REO agent make?

Listing REO (foreclosures) properties is my specialty, and you can make great money as an REO agent. If you are an established REO agent, you can sell well over 100 houses per year. REO listing commissions vary, as I receive 3 percent on some sales and as low as 1 percent on others. On average, I receive about 2.5 percent on each REO I sell. When I sell REOs, they typically sell for less than the average sales price in that area. If I assume the average price is $120,000, then multiply that by 100 houses at 2.5 percent commission, and assume I get a 90 percent split for selling that many houses, I earn $270,000 per year.

REO agent expenses are much higher than those for a typical listing agent. To be successful in REO, you must belong to REO organizations, register with REO companies, carry more insurance, and pay bank expenses on the properties. Often, you will have to eat some expenses and pay fees to cover the bank's bills (which isn't logical, but that is the deal). REO agents also attend conferences to meet clients and gain business. I attend at least two conferences per year. I estimate most REO agents pay at least $20,000 in expenses each year.

Let's say you manage to sell 100 houses per year. If that happens, handling everything yourself will be virtually impossible. Most likely, you will need at least one full-time assistant who will cost approximately $30,000 annually. Factor that into the expenses mentioned earlier, and your income drops to $220,000. Building that much sales volume isn't easy, and banks will not hand out listings to everyone who applies. There is also a lot of competition in the REO world. I have a coaching program available for those looking to get into the REO business. You are welcome to send me an email for more information. *Mark@investfourmore.com*

Working with short sales

When a homeowner sells their house for less than it is worth, it's called a short sale. Some banks or other lenders will agree to a short sale because it takes less time and may save them money over completing a foreclosure. The listing agent must help the sellers list the house like a traditional listing, but the agent also must help the seller communicate with the bank. The bank will need the seller to provide a ton of paperwork and may take weeks or even months to decide to accept an offer. Short sales come with many tax and legal implications, and agents must be familiar with those implications.

If an area has many houses in default, short sales can be a great way for agents to make money. However, short sales take a lot of work and patience. Working with banks is not always easy, and these situations can be very frustrating for the buyers and sellers.

Completing BPOs

BPOs (Broker Price Opinions) are like an appraisal and are completed by licensed agents. However, appraisals can only be completed by licensed appraisers and are much more detailed than a BPO. A BPO is a report used to value houses and consists of three recent sales and active-comparable houses that are similar to the property being valued. The BPO also includes commentary and other statistics. BPOs require an inspection, with some requiring only exterior pictures and others requiring interior photos. Real estate agents earn $30 to over $100 for completing BPOs.

Some agents make $50,000 or more simply doing BPOs. I complete many BPOs myself, but it is not my primary business. If you want to be a HUD or REO listing broker, you will have to complete many BPOs.

Property managers

Property managers manage rental properties for investors or other homeowners. They find renters, manage maintenance and repairs, collect rent, and keep track of accounting. Property managers usually get paid a monthly percentage of the rents collected (10 percent is common). They also charge leasing fees or other fees associated with the management of properties. To earn significant money as a property manager, you must have many properties. The best part about being a property manager is you can create consistent monthly income.

Many property managers also own maintenance and cleaning companies that they use for their properties. In most states, this relationship must be disclosed to the property owner.

Commercial real estate

Commercial real estate is an entirely different business than residential real estate. To learn the trade, many commercial agents will work at a large firm and may work for a salary, while residential agents typically work for commissions. Commercial properties can sell for much more than residential properties, but the sale can take a great deal of time. Selling commercial real estate takes much more knowledge due to the valuation process, which is much more involved. Instead of using the comparable-sales approach, which is used for most residential properties, commercial properties are valued based on their income and expenses.

Many commercial real estate companies require agents to have a degree in real estate, and it can take years to learn the business.

Running a real estate team

Running a team is one of the most profitable ways to make money in real estate. The key to long-term wealth is setting up a business that can run without the business owner and still make money. Becoming an agent and creating a team is one of the easiest ways to start a business. I run a team consisting of buyer's agents and staff to help me and the buyer's agents. As the team leader, I get a cut of each sale. I also pay many of the members' expenses and advertising costs, but their sales more than make up for those expenses.

Building your business to the point where you can add agents takes time, but it is well worth it. To run a team, you also need a reason for agents to join your team. I offer many buyer leads through my REO listings, and we use many other techniques to generate leads. I have a full-time contract manager who can write contracts for agents and help them communicate with lenders and title companies. The more listings an agent has, the more buyer leads you will earn from your listings. That is another reason it is nice to be a listing agent and not a buyer's agent.

How much money can a real estate agent make from running a team?

If you want to be successful, you can't hire help soon enough. The more people you hire, the more money you make while doing less work. It is a beautiful thing!

My team of 10 includes 6 licensed agents, although they don't all sell numerous houses. Most of my staff is licensed, even if they work behind the scenes. I provide incentive by giving them leads, paying some of their expenses, and providing staff to help them with paperwork. My team is set up so agents under me can sell houses easily and get paid. Starting a team is much easier if you have a lot of listings because listings bring in many buyer leads.

Following is a hypothetical breakdown of my annual earnings assuming I have three agents who are actively selling houses. Typically, agents earn 70 percent commission from their own clients and 50 percent from the leads I provide. Assume average house prices of $175,000, average commission of 3 percent, 90 percent cut from my broker, and 75 houses sold (50 percent from my leads and 50 percent from my agents' own clients).

For my leads that math comes to:

$175,000 average sale x 37.5 (half of 75 houses sold) x 3 percent commission x 90 percent split with broker x 50 percent split with me =$88,593.75.

For my agents' own leads the math is:

$175,000 x 37.5 x 3 percent x 90 percent x 30 percent =$53,156.25

My expenses may add up to $35,000, but my gross profits are $140,000 and my net profits are $100,000. Each agent earned approximately $65,000 per year, and I covered most of their expenses. It works out great for everyone as I make money for doing very little work and the agents get leads and paid expenses.

The great part about a real estate team is you can keep adding agents and making more money without increasing your own work load. Teams may be structured very differently, as some may do a 50/50 split for every deal. Other teams may not pay any expenses yet may give their agents a bigger cut.

Real estate broker

Every agent, if they're not a broker themselves, must work under a managing broker. Brokers oversee all agents in the office and run the office. Brokers must ensure everyone is acting legally and must take care of any disputes or problems. Some brokers run large offices with hundreds of agents, and some brokers just have a couple of agents. Most states require real estate agents to be licensed for a certain amount of time before they can be a broker.

Managing brokers may be hired by the owner of the company and make a salary or a percentage of the sales in the office. The managing broker is often the company owner and gets a percentage of their agents' commissions as well as desk fees or advertising money from their agents. Real estate offices are run in many different ways, and just about every broker does things a little differently.

Saving money as an agent

If you also want to be a real estate investor, being an agent offers a huge advantage. A licensed agent saves money on commissions when they buy and sell houses, and it helps them find more deals. I estimate being an agent saved me over $70,000 on my own deals every year. I have purchased 16 long-term rentals, and I also flip 10 to 15 houses per year. I've realized the benefits of being an agent, and some investors become agents simply to focus on their own personal investing.

Conclusion

If you want to become a real estate agent, don't pay attention to the average or median income statistics. I personally earn money from my team, REO listings, BPOs, and the few buyers and sellers I work with personally. Getting to this point takes time, but with hard work, it can be done. I won't tell you exactly how much money I make every year, but many agents across the country make over $1 million. The top agent in the country sold 1,099 houses last year! We are talking millions and millions in commissions in just one year, and I know that agent had other people doing most of the work for him. For agents who are just starting out, the next chapter covers what to expect your first year.

CHAPTER 2

How Much Money Do Real Estate Agents Make in Their First Year?

Being an agent is a great way to make a living, but getting started isn't easy. Building a client base and earning income takes time. In fact, building a large client base can take years. It is important to have an idea of how much a real estate agent will make in their first year so you can plan how much money you need to save before getting started. Having said that, some go-getter agents can make over $100,000 in their first year. Two agents on my team did, but those results are not typical.

What does the average agent make in their first year?

Average-income statistics for an agent's first year are hard to find. I did find some information, but it is from 2006! Even though these statistics are old, I think we can still use them.

The National Association of Realtors (NAR) conducted a survey in 2006 that reported Realtors with fewer than two years of experience earned a median income of $15,300. A Realtor is slightly different from an agent because they belong to NAR and work by a specific code of ethics (Realtor and real estate agent income should be very similar). Even though this data is 10 years old, the median income for all Realtors in 2006 was $47,000, and the median income for all Realtors in 2014 was $45,700. Since the median income for Realtors is almost identical, it is safe to assume the average income for new agents is similar.

Since the data covered Realtors with fewer than two years of experience, the actual average income for agents in their first year is most likely less than $15,000. Please don't get scared off by that statistic!

Why average income can be misleading

Some agents will make much more than the $15,000 figure. If an agent has a plan, sets goals, and follows through with their plan, they can easily make $30,000 in their first year.

I like to look at the positive side and think a new agent who works hard can make $50,000 in their first year. Most people don't plan, don't set goals, don't take chances, and don't go after what they really want. That doesn't mean you shouldn't plan to make a lot less.

Many agents start out part-time to test the waters. Part-time agents do not earn much money. If you have another job, realizing success in real estate is very tough, and your income may not meet your expectations. Many agents quit during their first year because they don't make as much money as they expected. This is usually because they aren't willing to jump in full time. While the statistics show agents do not make much money in their first year, in reality, most agents don't try very hard.

How much money did I make in my first year?

I made over $40,000 in my first year, but I had a lot of help. My father was an agent and helped me get into the business. I also helped my father complete fix and flips during my first year, which helped me increase my income. Having said that, I did not work very hard to sell houses on the real estate side of the business. If I could do it over again, I could make well over $50,000 in my first year knowing what I know now about marketing, follow up, and networking.

Selling real estate is not rocket science: the more contacts you have, the more houses you will sell. The secret is building a client base that will continue to buy houses from you and refer people to you. 84 percent of buyers and sellers said they would recommend and use their agent again. Therefore, once you get a client and do a decent job for them, they will continue to use you and tell their friends about you.

The trick is finding people who will use you. In your first year, it is especially difficult because no one knows you are an agent. You must tell everyone that you are an agent, or better yet, that you are becoming an agent. If you tell everyone you know you are becoming an agent, you can build your client base before becoming one.

Conclusion

Do not be shy, and do not worry that you don't know what you are doing. If you want to be an agent, you must educate yourself, but education alone won't earn you money. The best way to educate yourself is to learn by doing and gaining experience. Agents that make $100,000 in their first year don't worry about being perfect—they worry about meeting people and selling houses.

CHAPTER 3

How Much Money Do You Need to Save before Becoming a Real Estate Agent?

When you become an agent, you give up a steady paycheck, and making money takes a while in most cases. Unless you can start as an assistant making an hourly wage, you must save money before you become an agent. It could be one, three, or six months before you sell a house and earn a commission check. This is why many agents try to start out part time. However, if you try to work part time, it will be tough to make it unless you have a very flexible schedule or additional help.

One reason earning money takes time is closing on a house takes a long time. Once a house goes under contract, it usually takes 30 to 40 days for that house to sell. If an agent is able to close a deal right after they get their license, they will not get paid until at least one month later.

It can also take an agent several months (or longer) to get their license. If a potential agent decides to quit their job before they get their license, they'll go a couple of months without receiving a paycheck.

It also takes time to build up business. At the beginning, an agent's circle of influence is the best opportunity for making sales. Friends and family are the easiest targets, but they may not be in the market to buy or sell right away. Finding buyers or sellers can take months, and then you have to wait for properties to close.

How long does it take an agent to start making consistent money?

The key to being a successful agent is getting leads. The more leads you get, the more people become your clients and the more sales you'll have. I have seen new agents attack real estate with everything they have. Those agents closed one or two deals per month by their second or third month in the business.

After six months, they really start to take off and realize consistent monthly sales and income.

I have also seen agents get stuck educating themselves and doing prep work for months without going after business. It takes them a year or longer to start making consistent money, and some give up before they make it. I have also seen agents who were afraid to talk on the phone and tried to do everything at their office on their computer. Real estate is about meeting and talking to people. Talking to people isn't easy for everyone, but if you want to be successful in life, you must do what isn't easy. Because everyone is different, it's hard to say if it will take three or six months for an agent to make enough money to support themselves. Generally, I'd plan on it taking 6 months.

Remember, there is no better way to learn the business than to start working with clients right away. The more people you talk to about being an agent, the better chance you have of making sales.

How much money will you need to be successful?

Not only do you have to worry about working for months before you start making money, but you must also spend money to make money. An agent's expenses will depend on their agreement with their broker. Some brokers will help an agent with costs like MLS dues, board dues, and advertising. Other brokers will not pay for anything yet offer a larger commission split.

If you have no way to save money before becoming an agent, there are ways to make money immediately by working on a team, which we will get into later.

An agent will most likely have to pay for E and O insurance, MLS fees, advertising, marketing materials, business cards, mailings, office fees, and the cost of getting a license. This assumes an agent has the basic materials needed like a smart phone, laptop, desk, chairs, and other supplies.

Here are the bare-minimum costs a new agent will pay:
Obtain license: $1,000
Initial marketing: $500
Insurance: $200
MLS and board dues: $200
Total: $1,900

And here are the bare-minimum monthly costs:
Marketing: $250
Insurance: $40
MLS and board dues: $50
Office fees: $200
Total: $540

These are the minimum costs needed to get started, and these costs vary from state to state and market to market. Always research these costs before you make the decision to become an agent. Talk to other agents and brokers in your market to see what their costs are. You will also be driving much more, and consequently, you will have higher fuel costs. You may have to take clients out to lunch or dinner. You even may have to purchase for-sale signs or name riders.

How much money do you need to save before you become an agent?

Make a realistic plan and calculate your costs based on that. Your plan should include your expected timeline for when you start making money and how much you will spend on marketing and expenses. Generally, I would save 6 months of living expenses. That does not include the initial start-up costs like getting your license. While that may seem extreme, I have seen too many agents start in the business, get momentum, and then quit because they ran out of money.

CHAPTER 4

Why a Real Estate Career is Better Than a Corporate Job

I have been an agent for quite some time. In fact, I don't feel like it is possible for me to be old enough to have been in the business for 15 years. I have accomplished a lot in my life, and I am not close to being finished. When I was growing up, I always said I would never be a real estate agent. My dad became an agent in 1978, right before I was born, and I grew up in his office. I remember sleeping under his desk when I was three or four. I didn't mind hanging out with him, and he made good money, but for some reason, I never wanted to follow in his footsteps. I don't think logic told me to avoid real estate, but instead, my young male ego said I should make my own way!

Coming out of college, I had the choice of joining the corporate world or working with my father. In college, I was taught to get a corporate job, invest in the stock market, and if I worked really hard, I could retire in about 40 years. Maybe if I worked 100 hours per week for 20 years, I could become a CFO or CEO and make the big bucks. Working 100 hours per week for someone else never appealed to me, but I didn't know how to start my own business. In the end, I decided not to join the corporate world and instead joined my father's real estate team. I did not choose real estate because I spent time researching the pros and cons; it was more a choice of convenience. I couldn't find a job out of college that paid what I thought I was worth, and my dad offered me a job in real estate, where I knew I could make decent money. After seeing how my friends in the corporate world are treated compared to what it's like to run my own business, I am extremely happy things worked out the way they did.

I lucked into an awesome career, but you don't have to. You can make the choice to become an agent, and if you dedicate yourself from the beginning, you can be very successful very quickly.

A career in real estate offers more freedom than a corporate job

Real estate agents have a lot of freedom. Most agents are their own boss and make their own schedule. They can work as much or as little as they want, which is a good thing for many people but can be a challenge for others. You must have a great work ethic to create business. Agents either work under a broker or are their own broker, but that broker is not exactly their boss. The agent is usually a self-employed contractor and not an employee. That means they set their own schedule, take vacations when they want, take time off to watch their kids' plays or recitals, and choose when and how much they work. Agents have a lot of freedom, but they also must be disciplined enough to work hard and smartly without someone telling them what to do.

I think most of us know how the corporate world works. You work your butt off to rise through the company ranks. You get raises with each promotion, and you usually take on more responsibility and more work. You work for a salary; your hours are dictated by your boss, and they can be daunting. I know many successful people in the corporate world who work 60, 70, or 80 hours per week! Since they are salaried workers, they don't make more money for all the extra hours they put in. Hopefully, at some point, they will be rewarded for that hard work with another promotion.

A promotion may mean more money, but it also means even longer hours and less time with your family. At some point 20 years down the road, you may become a top-level manager or CEO. That assumes the company you work for still exists and you enjoy working 80-hour weeks for the 20 years leading up to that "dream job." That "dream job" probably means you now get to work 100 hours per week and take on even more responsibility. The crazy thing is I was taught to take this route in college. They made it seem both glamorous and the expected thing to do when you graduate. Thank goodness I did not listen to my teachers and chose my own route instead of the corporate route.

Does a real estate career allow you to make more money than a corporate job?

Many people see the average agent's income ($40,000, remember?) and assume agents don't make much money. But those statistics count part-time agents and agents who treat their job as a hobby. I mentioned agents must motivate themselves and make themselves work hard. Not everyone can or will work hard unless they have a boss telling them what to do. Our office has over 50 agents now, and I see about 10 of them on a consistent basis. Most work from home or barely work at all, and they greatly skew the average-income figure.

Agents who spend time on the business and work intelligently make a lot of money. It is not uncommon to see an agent make well over $100,000 per year. Our office has at least four agents making well over $100,000 and two who make over $300,000 year after year. The top agents in our area (which is not a massive metropolitan area) make over $1 million per year. While the average income for agents is low, there is no ceiling for good agents. You make your own way and are rewarded for the work you put in because you are your own boss. You do not have to rely on someone else to see the effort, the intelligence, and the potential.

There are some misconceptions about how long it takes to build a real estate business. It did not take all those agents 20 years to build up their business. My team has two agents who made over $100,000 in their first year. This is not typical, and I don't want people to think they will make that much money right away, but it is possible. I know a couple in Arizona who made over $1 million in real estate two years after becoming agents! The other great thing about being an agent is you can build your own team. You can hire staff and agents who will sell houses for you. Instead of being the worker in the corporate world, you can be the boss and start your own business. Since my team of 10 does most of the work, I'm free to invest, write for my blog, and spend time with my family while still making a great income.

You can make a lot of money in the corporate world as well, but you do not have the freedom or control you have with real estate. I know a few corporate people who make six figures, and they get benefits like health insurance. Because agents are self-employed, they don't enjoy the same benefits as corporate workers. Anyone entering the field should account for this. The corporate people I know who make good money have been working crazy hours for years. They also find themselves running into a pay ceiling once they make it to that six-figure income. There is a lot of competition in the corporate world, and you must be the best of the best to earn six figures. Plus, once you reach a certain age in the corporate world, you face the problem of younger and cheaper talent replacing you. My good friend left the corporate world (where he was a top-level manager) for these reasons. He learned about real estate from me. In less than two years, he has reached the same income he earned at the end of his ten-year corporate career.

Real estate forces you to run your own businesses

We have all heard the best way to get rich is to start your own business. Real estate is one of the easiest businesses to start and has a very high profit potential. In real estate, you need very little capital to get started, customers are easy to find, marketing is relatively cheap, and you need few assets. If you want to be a real estate agent, you must treat it as a business...not a job. You must be the boss, make big goals, plan well, work hard, and keep yourself motivated. If you expect everything to fall in your lap without doing any real work, you are going to be very disappointed.

In the corporate world, you have no chance to start your own business. You constantly work for someone else, making money for their business. Usually, you have no time or flexibility to create something on the side, and you get stuck in a rut that can last for years. Many people prefer the corporate world because they have someone telling them exactly what to do and when to do it. Real estate is not for everyone.

When you are your own boss, nothing is planned for you. You don't have hours you must keep, and no one tells you what to do and when to do it. Many people like having their lives planned for them because it easier than taking control. To get the most out of life, you must be in control. You must make your own schedule, plan for your future, plan your own retirement, plan vacations, and plan exciting things to do.

As both an agent and business owner, I can keep hiring people and grow my business as big as I want. The only ceiling is the one I put on myself. As I grow, I can keep hiring staff to meet increased workloads. I keep growing and hiring more people every year, and I actually work less now than I did a few years ago. The staff I hire takes care of the increased management that more staff requires.

A real estate career can be more stable than a corporate job

Most people assume a corporate job is "safer" than being your own boss. You will receive a steady check, benefits, and a clear path for your future. However, who controls your future in the corporate world? Can you hire or fire yourself? Do you have control over the company's success? Can you control whether the company is sold or not? What happens if the technology your company thrives on becomes obsolete?

If things go bad in the corporate world, will they take care of you? No. They will let you go to cut costs and make more money. They will let you go because they can hire someone with less experience and pay them less to do the same job. A corporate job has no security because you have no guarantees you will have a job in the future. If you are your own boss, you make all the decisions and decide if you succeed or fail and how long you will be employed.

A real estate career allows you to invest in real estate more easily

I love investing in real estate because I earn over 15 percent cash on cash returns on my rentals and earn half of my income from fix and flips. I wouldn't have the time and knowledge I do if I had to work full time in another job. I have a very flexible schedule that allows me to look at great deals anytime I want, and I can make an offer within hours. This gives me a huge advantage over other investors who must work during the day.

Being in the real estate industry also allows me to have connections and networking opportunities that help me make more money as an investor. Plus, I save commission fees by acting as my own agent when buying and selling properties.

CHAPTER 5

Is the Real Estate Industry in Trouble Thanks to New Technology?

Many people think websites like Zillow and Trulia are going to replace real estate agents, much like online travel sites replaced travel agents. I read forum posts or receive emails explaining why agents are paid too much and why the industry must change or technology will destroy it. While technology has made the house buying and selling process easier, I don't think people realize how valuable real estate agents are. The biggest value an agent brings is not the hours they spend taking pictures, marketing a house, or writing contracts. The biggest value an agent offers is experience pricing houses and negotiating and getting their buyer or seller the best deal possible. The tricky part about real estate is every single house is different. The more experience someone has, the better they can value, market, and negotiate, which online sites do not do well.

I think it is important for prospective or current agents to know why Zillow is not going to destroy our industry. Real estate agents are too valuable, and as I've discussed, agents are responsible for a lot. It is not feasible for most homeowners or buyers to take over the agent's job.

How are online real estate sites changing the real estate industry?

Many people use Zillow, Realtor.com, Redfin, Trulia, and other national websites to value their houses, find listings, and get real estate related information. These sites have made it much easier for consumers to find houses for sale and determine the value of their own house. Many people feel that these sites can easily replace agents because consumers no longer need to rely on an agent to list their house, market it, or find a new house. While the general public can use these sites to find houses for sale, value houses, and market houses, that does not mean it is a smart move.

Besides determining value and finding houses for sale, a lot goes into the buying and selling process. Real estate agents handle the contracts, paperwork, marketing, negotiations, and showings. One more thing to consider is that the large sites may offer values and listings, but that does not mean their values are correct or that they are showing all available houses for sale.

The large, national websites that list houses for sale use syndication to bring those listings to the general public. Zillow does not own that information, and the information is not public either because the pictures and listing descriptions are copyrighted material. Many people do not realize that by using only those sites for their real estate information, they are not getting the full picture. Here are some issues with the national websites and the data they deliver:

- The national websites that use syndication don't show you every house for sale in the MLS. Many people do not know this, but Zillow and other sites have to get permission from real estate agents and MLS systems to market those properties. While it appears Zillow has all available houses on their site, not all agents and MLS systems agree to list their properties on Zillow.

- The national syndication sites also do not update their information as quickly as the MLS does. Information on Zillow can be days behind on price changes, houses under contract, and new listings. We get calls from buyers asking about listings on Zillow that they think are available yet have been under contract for days.

- The agent listed on the properties on the national sites are not always the listing agents. Many of the sites that list properties for sale also show real estate agent information along with those properties. While it may appear that the agent listed is the listing agent, most of those agents pay to be listed on the website and have no affiliation with that property.

- The values given by Zillow and other sites can be extremely inaccurate. Prices can easily be 20 percent higher or lower than the actual value, and many consumers assume the value estimates are accurate.

Pricing your house too high or too low can cause the seller to lose a lot of money. In most cases, pricing your house incorrectly will cost you much more than the real estate commission you were trying to save.

- If you are using large syndication websites to look for houses, you are most likely missing out on listings that are for sale but not on those sites. You are also getting outdated information and inaccurate property values.

Why do people think real estate agents will become obsolete?

Zillow and other sites have stated they have no interest in becoming real estate brokerages. However, there is still a large portion of the population that feels these sites will become real estate listing services where sellers can list their houses for sale and buyers can purchase them. They feel that real estate agents will have to drastically reduce the commissions they charge or consumers will sell houses themselves and leave agents out of the business. Here is why I both think that will not happen and the system will not change much in the near future.

- We know how inaccurate computer-generated values can be. All real estate is different, and part of a real estate agent's value is knowing how to price houses correctly. Price a house too low and you leave thousands on the table. Price it too high, and it will sit on the market and cost the seller thousands because the listing becomes stagnant. Statistics from NAR show for-sale-by-owner (FSBO) houses sell for much less and take much longer to sell than houses listed by a real estate agent. FSBOs accounted for 8% of sales in 2014. **The typical FSBO house sold for $210,000 compared to $249,000 for agent-assisted sales.** These statistics include homeowners who used the MLS and online marketing to advertise their house as for sale by owner.
- If you use a website like Zillow to sell your house, the buyer will have to handle all the tasks associated with selling the house:
  - Showings

- Paperwork
- Negotiation
- Finding a title company
- Marketing
- Inspections
- Appraisals
- Much more

One of the biggest factors affecting for-sale-by-owner properties is that real estate agents usually do not charge the buyer anything. The seller pays for both the listing agent and the buyer's agent commissions. Why in the world would a buyer avoid using an agent if it costs them nothing? When a seller tries to sell without an agent, they are stuck without representation, while the buyer will have representation. If they don't want to pay for the buyer's agent, they will severely limit the number of buyers who will look at their house, which costs the seller money. If the seller pays for the buyer's agent and the marketing, and if they consider all the time they must spend digesting contracts and setting up showings, they aren't even saving any money. That does not take into consideration that the buyer's agent has a professional working on their side who is better at negotiating and is experienced at selling houses. This is why for-sale-by-owner houses sell for so much less than regular listings.

While there are real estate agents who charge low fees to list a house on the MLS, sellers still run into the same problems because they lack agent representation. If you get into legal trouble, are you going to hire the cheapest lawyer you can find because they are all the same? No. You hire the best lawyer you can afford. If you are selling the most valuable thing you will ever own, do you want to try to sell it yourself or use the cheapest real estate agent you can find? You want to use the best agent you can afford so that you get the most money for your house.

Why can't sellers use an appraisal to value their house and save money on real estate commissions?

I also hear the argument that a real estate appraiser, instead of an agent, can be used to value a house. While real estate appraisers value houses, the main objective of an appraisal is to verify value—not determine it. Banks use appraisals to verify that a house is worth at least as much as it's under contract for.

After the last housing crisis, the entire appraisal system was changed to stop inflated and fraudulent appraisals. This has made appraisers very wary of appraising houses too high. This is why an appraisal on a house you are buying, no matter how good of a deal it is, will almost always come in right at or slightly above the contract price. When you refinance a house, you will also find appraisals tend to come in lower than market value because appraisers are being careful not to come in too high and risk being investigated.

Appraisers also do not use active-comparable properties to value houses; they only use sold comparables. By definition, appraisers are not supposed to value houses higher than comparable sold properties, even in a very hot market. If an appraiser runs into a property with very few sold properties to compare it to, the appraiser can have a very hard time valuing the property. Many times, appraisers ask us for comparable properties and ideas on how to value the property. A real estate agent actually has more flexibility when valuing properties and can use active comparable properties and market trends to more accurately determine values. Agents can also help prevent low appraisals by providing appraisers with sold comparable properties.

Will the real estate sales industry evolve?

I believe the real estate industry will evolve, and agents will have to change with it. Agents will have to become more tech savvy. They will have to learn to use syndication websites and explain their benefits and downfalls, and they will have to be able to explain their value. Sellers always tell me about how they sold their house on their own in one day and saved $6,000 in real estate agent commissions. If they sold their house in one day, they probably underpriced it and cost themselves at least $10,000.

If you sell a house yourself using one of the large syndication websites or by paying a low fee to put your house in the MLS, do you really save money? On the surface, it may look like you are saving on commission, but in reality, you are most likely leaving money on the table by not valuing your house correctly or knowing how to negotiate. On top of that, you have to wade through the contracts, marketing, and showings yourself. I believe most people realize listing houses themselves is not worth the time, effort, or possible loss of money, and that is why the real estate sales industry has not changed very much.

Other industries that have changed, like travel agents, stock brokers, and even car dealerships, have done so because almost anyone can look up the value of those goods or commodities and be fairly certain what the market value is. Because every piece of real estate is different, it is much harder to value, and valuing a property incorrectly can be a huge mistake.

PART II

CHAPTER 6

How Hard Is It to Become a Real Estate Agent?

If you are thinking of getting your real estate license, you may be asking yourself: how hard is it? That is a difficult question to answer because each state has different licensing laws and requirements. However, a good friend of mine just passed the real estate test in Colorado, and I have some great information from him on what to expect here. This information may not apply to your state, but it will give you an idea of what is involved. Some states have fewer requirements and some have more. I have had my license for over 15 years, and it was not easy to obtain. Plus, things have become even more difficult over the years.

How much time does it take?

In Colorado, you must currently take 162 hours of real estate classes before you can take the real estate exam. That is over four weeks assuming 40 hours of classes per week. Most people don't have the time to devote 40 hours per week to real estate school. It took my friend 8 months to take the classes and pass his real estate test. He had a full-time job and was forced to take classes after work and on the weekends. He took his real estate classes online so that he could have a flexible schedule. Most states have much fewer required hours, but some have more. In Texas, you need 210 hours of classes.

What is involved?

There is more to getting your real estate license than taking classes and passing a test. Real estate is a highly regulated industry, and these are some of the other requirements in Colorado (most states have very similar requirements):

- You must pass a background test, which involves being fingerprinted.

- You must pass tests and quizzes to go along with the 162 hours of classes. Getting your license in Colorado is no walk in the park. As my friend Justin said, "Reading dry material at night after work and after family time was rough. I was usually tired. The tests at the end of each section were very difficult. They would ask about minute details. My school didn't even try to make it interesting or add commentary—they pretty much copied and pasted out of the Colorado legal documents on the topics."
- Once you pass the exam, you must hang your license with a broker and pass the background check to activate your license.
- You must buy E and O insurance, and you most likely will want to become a Realtor, join a local board, and join a local multiple listing service (MLS). Becoming an agent isn't cheap.
- Once you have your license, you must take 24 hours of continuing education every three years to keep your license active.

What are real estate classes like?

You can take real estate courses online or in person. My friend, Justin, took the classes online to make it easier to plan around his busy work schedule. In my and my friend's experience, taking real estate classes online is extremely boring since staring at a computer for 168 hours is not easy. Here is what Justin had to say about his experience:

"If I could do it over again I would take the classes in person—if that fits your lifestyle. In person would have been more engaging and exciting. Online is good for flexibility of hours, but that's about it. The material is pretty dry, so it's exhausting reading that much on a computer screen for that long. Some online schools are starting to do video-based instruction. I personally would put this in last place. With written material, you can move at your own place and easily copy/paste and review sections as needed. Video would be at a determined pace, and you'd have to manually take notes."

I took the classes online 15 years ago, and I struggled to get through them. I had been around real estate my whole life, and I still had a hard time reading all that information online.

The material is very dry. If you hope to learn how to invest in real estate or learn advanced house-selling techniques, think again! The material covers technical laws, procedures, settlement sheets, and case history. Material that will help people sell houses or help you personally invest in real estate is scarce. The material is meant to keep people from going to jail for committing fraud or misleading buyers and sellers, not to actually help you succeed.

What is the Colorado real estate test like?

The Colorado real estate test is not easy! To tell the truth, I failed it twice myself, even though I thought I would breeze through it. Many of the questions are very tricky, with double negatives and wording meant to trick you. You also must memorize a ton, and you need to be able to do math for the settlement sheets! The test is about memorization and your ability to take tests. It takes up to four hours, is conducted in a high-security test center, and you aren't allowed to bring notes.

My friend passed the test on his first try, but as he says, he is used to taking exams like this. He has his MBA and has taken many similar professional exams in his previous corporate career.

How much does it cost to get your real estate license?

In Colorado, the cost of real estate courses varies widely. Some online schools cost as little as a few hundred dollars, while classroom courses can run into the thousands. Currently, the exam itself costs $80, and you must also pay an accredited company or a law-enforcement office to fingerprint you. Once you get your license, you will have continued costs, like board dues, MLS dues, operating expenses, and fee or commission splits to pay your broker. Do not be surprised when you learn it costs a couple thousand dollars per year to stay on as an active agent.

How hard is it to become a real estate agent?

If you want to become a real estate agent, make sure you research your state's requirements. Some states have easier requirements than others, but regardless of the state, the process is rarely easy. It may cost you significant time and money, but in my opinion, it is well worth it. Being an agent saves me a ton of money and offers me a better opportunity to buy properties below market value. I consider those bonuses on top of the incredible income you can earn from real estate.

The great things in life are never easy. Often, the more work it takes to accomplish something, the better it feels when you accomplish it. Don't think of how hard it will be. Instead, think of how awesome of a challenge it will be...and how great it will feel once you make it big.

CHAPTER 7

What Are the Real Estate Licensing Requirements in Most States?

Every state has different requirements. Each requires some form of education and a test you must pass. You must also work under a broker initially. State requirements for education vary from 20 credit hours to over 200 hours.

Every state has a different system for licensing real estate agents and real estate brokers. In most states, there are real estate salespeople and real estate brokers. A real estate salesperson must work under a real estate broker in order to be an active licensee. To become a broker, most states requires you to work a certain amount of time as a salesperson and pursue additional education and testing. Some states, like Colorado, have different names for brokers and salespeople. Here, new agents are called broker associates. Additionally, Colorado has employing brokers or independent brokers.

What are each state's license requirements?

In this section, I list every state and include their requirements for an entry-level license. Many states require background checks, fingerprints, and a high school diploma. Background checks are subjective in each state. Many states say you can't have a felony, but each case will be looked at for extenuating circumstances. If you are already licensed in one state, most other states will not require nearly as much education for obtaining a license in their state (this is called "reciprocation").

This information was up to date as of 2015, but some states may have changed their requirements. There is also a very small chance I could have made an error gathering this data. Make sure you check with your state for the actual requirements.

Alabama:

In Alabama, you must be a U.S. citizen or lawful permanent resident, be at least 19 years old, show proof of high school graduation or a GED, have no felonies, have not had a real estate application or license rejected or revoked in any state within the past two years, successfully complete 60 approved credits of pre-license Alabama real estate courses, and pass real estate license exams.

Licensees must also complete a 30-hour real estate agent training program within the first twelve months of getting their license.

Alaska:

Alaska has three different types of real estate licenses: salesperson, broker, and broker associate. The salesperson must work under a broker and is required to have 40 pre-license credit hours plus pass the real estate exam. You must be 19 years of age, and people with felonies must have served their full sentence.

Arizona:

You must be 18 years of age and complete 90 hours of pre-license education. You must pass the state and real estate school exams plus be of high moral character.

Arkansas:

You must be 18 years old and take 60 hours of pre-license education. You must also take a background check, which is assessed on a case-by-case scenario.

California:

Applicants in California are only required to take three real estate classes, which can be taken at a college or a private real estate school. Applicants must also show proof of honesty and truthfulness. Conviction of any crime can result in disqualification.

Colorado:

You must take 162 credit hours before you can take the state exams. You must also pass a background test and be fingerprinted.

Connecticut:

You must take 60 hours of real estate classes before you can take the exam for a salesperson. Brokers must take 120 hours and have 2 years' experience as a salesperson.

Delaware:

Licensees in Delaware must complete 99 hours of real estate classes before they can take the state exam.

District of Columbia:

In the District of Colombia, you must take 60 hours of pre-license education.

Florida:

You must take 63 credit hours of pre-license courses and be at least 18 years of age as well as have a high school diploma or equivalent.

Georgia:

For a salesperson license, Georgia requires 75 hours of approved pre-licensure real estate courses, or 10 quarter hours or 6 semester hours of approved education courses at an accredited college or university. You must also be 18 years of age and pass a background check.

Hawaii:

You must be 21 years old and pass a real estate pre-licensing course. Hawaii does not list the number of credit hours in their courses, but I did some research, and it appears to be about 60 hours' worth of classes.

Idaho:

You must be 18 years of age and take 90 hours of pre-license education before you can take the state exam.

Illinois:

You must be 21 years old and have either a high school diploma or a GED. The pre-license real estate education requirement is 45 hours, and in some cases applicants as young as 18 may be accepted.

Indiana:

Indiana requires applicants to be 18 years old and to not have been convicted of a crime that indicates they may endanger the public. You must take 54 credit hours of pre-license classes and pass the state exam.

Iowa:

You must be 18 years old and pass a background check. You are only required to take 36 credit hours of pre-license classes before taking the state exam.

Kansas:

You must be 18 years old and have a high school diploma or its equivalent. You only need 30 hours of pre-license classes before taking the exam.

Kentucky:

You must be 18 years old, have a high school diploma or equivalent, and pass a background check. You must take 96 credit hours before you can take the state exam.

Louisiana:

You must be 18 years old and have a high school diploma or equivalent. You must take 90 hours of pre-license education before you can take the state exams.

Maine:

Maine requires you to be 18 years old, have a high school diploma or GED, and have notarized recommendations from at least 3 persons stating that you have a good reputation. You must take 55 hours of pre-licensing requirements before taking the real estate license exams.

Maryland:

You must be 18 years old and of good character and reputation. You must take 60 hours of pre-licensing education before you can take the real estate license exam.

Massachusetts:

You must be 18 years old and take 24 credit hours of classes before you can take the state exam.

Michigan:

You must be 18 years old and take 40 hours of pre-license education before you can take the state exams.

Minnesota:

You must take three real estate classes to get your license. Only the first class must be passed before you can take the state test, and the other two classes must be passed within one year.

Mississippi

You must be 18 years old and a bona fide resident. You must complete 60 hours of pre-license education before taking the state exam.

Missouri:

In Missouri, you can get your license in a variety of ways. You must be 18 and complete 48 hours of classes; be a licensed attorney; or be granted a one-time sitting for the exam by the commission.

Montana:

You must be 18 years old and have passed the 10th grade. You also must take 60 hours of pre-license education before taking the real estate test.

Nebraska:

You must be 18 years old and have a high school diploma or GED. You must take 60 hours of continuing education before taking the state real estate exam.

Nevada:

You must take 90 hours of pre-license education before taking the state real estate exam.

New Hampshire:

You must be 18 and complete 40 hours of pre-license education before taking the real estate exam.

New Jersey:

You must be 18 years old and have a high school diploma or GED. You must pass 75 hours of pre-license classes before taking the real estate exam.

New Mexico:

You must be 18 years old and a legal resident of the United States. You must pass 90 hours of pre-license classes before taking the state real estate exam.

New York:

You must be 18 years old and take 75 hours of pre-license education before passing the state real estate exam.

North Carolina:

You must take 75 hours of pre-license classes before you can take the state real estate exam.

North Dakota:

You must be 18 years old and take 45 credit hours of pre-license education. The test can be taken before you finish the 45-hour pre-license education, but you must finish the education within one year.

Ohio:

You must be 18 years old, have a high school diploma, and be an honest and upright citizen. If you have had a felony, you may be denied a license. The applicant must pass a state real estate test and complete 120 hours of education.

Oklahoma:

You must be 18 years old and of good moral character. You must take 90 hours of pre-license education before taking your real estate exam.

Oregon:

You must be 18 years old and have a high school diploma or GED. You must take 150 hours of pre-license education before taking the real estate exam.

Pennsylvania:

You must take 60 credit hours of pre-license education or have a major in real estate from a four-year college.

Rhode Island:

You must be 18 years old and complete 45 hours of pre-license credits before you can take the state real estate test.

South Carolina:

In South Carolina, you must be 18 years old and have a high school diploma or equivalent. You must complete 60 hours of pre-license education before taking the state real estate exam. After passing the exam, you must also take an additional 30 hours of post-license education within your first year as an agent.

South Dakota:

You must be 18 years old and complete 116 hours of pre-license education before you can take the state real estate exams.

Tennessee:

You must be 18 years old and complete 60 hours of pre-license education before taking the real estate exam.

Texas:

You must complete 210 hours of pre-license education before you can take the real estate exam.

Utah:

Utah requires you to be 18 years old and requires a background check. You must complete 120 hours of pre-license education before taking the real estate exam.

Vermont:

You must be 18 and complete 40 hours of pre-license education before passing the state real estate tests.

Virginia:

You must be 18 years old and complete 60 hours of pre-license education prior to taking the state license exams.

Washington:

You must be 18 years old and complete 60 hours of education before taking the real estate tests.

West Virginia:

You must be 18 years old and have a high school diploma or equivalent. Applicants must take 90 hours of pre-license education before taking the state exams.

Wisconsin:

You must be 18 years old and have completed 72 hours of pre-license education before taking the state test. You can also be a real estate apprentice, which requires a general knowledge test and you to be working directly for a real estate broker for at least 20 hours per week.

Wyoming:

You need to take 54 credit hours of pre-license education before passing the state exams.

CHAPTER 8

Should You Take Real Estate Classes Online?

One of the hardest parts of getting your real estate license is completing the education needed for licensing requirements. In most states, you can take classes either online or in-person with a real teacher. There are many pros and cons to each, and your goals and plans for your future as an agent will determine which is better for you. I and many of my team members obtained the license online, but my wife got hers in a classroom. While getting your license online may be faster, it may not be your best option.

One of the pros of taking classes online is you may be able to finish the classes sooner than the actual hourly requirement. Each class is given a certain amount of hourly credits, and once you pass the class, you get credit for those hours. If someone is a fast learner or reader, it may only take them 2 hours instead of 4 to finish a section online. If you take classes in person, you must be in a classroom for very close to the full hourly requirement.

The downfall to taking real estate classes online is that they are extremely boring. Starting at a computer screen for hours and absorbing information that way is tough. No matter how hard you try, making real estate license material exciting is very difficult; in fact, most of it is extremely boring. You must have a very good attention span to spend time studying online material and then be able to pass the exam. In-person classes are much more exciting. You won't be staring at a computer screen. You will be listening to a teacher, reading books, and listening to guest speakers.

If you take online classes, you must also be self-motivated. You must find the time to sit down and put those hours in. In a classroom, you will have a set schedule and someone telling you when you need to be there. If you have a job and or family, finding time to take online classes is even tougher. Justin, who we talked about earlier, took 8 months to finish his classes! Part of that was because he had a job and a family. He took his classes online, and it was tough for him to make the time to study.

Is it better to learn real estate from a real person?

In-person real estate classes will have real people teaching you and learning with you. You will most likely learn much more from a real classroom because the teacher can explain many more things than a computer can. That teacher also should have some real-world experience and may even have connections in the real estate world.

When you become an agent, one of your most important tasks will be meeting people and networking. The sooner you can start networking, the better off you will be. Your teacher or teachers may have broker connections, insights on the best way to pass the test, and ways to help you get started selling houses! Real estate classes don't teach you how to sell—they teach you the laws, how to avoid being sued, and how to abide by ethics standards.

In-person classes are much more interesting than staring at a computer screen all day, but there are other advantages. I am a HUD broker, and I taught one of my HUD classes to a local community college that offered a real estate licensing program. I taught aspiring agents all about HUD homes, including things to watch out for and how to make money selling them. Online classes won't teach students the best way to sell HUD homes and won't have guest speakers.

The teacher may also bring in guest speakers and other agents who have succeeded in the business. An online class will not expose you to real estate agents who are succeeding in your area.

The teacher will also be able to tell stories and relate the law and rules to real-world examples. Online classes may be able to give some real-world examples, but it is always better to hear stories straight from the people who experienced them.

It may be difficult to find an in-person schedule that fits you. Online classes afford much more scheduling flexibility, but when you take in-person classes, you must make their schedule work. If you already have a job, that may be difficult to do, but many schools offer night classes to help work around students' schedules.

Which class format takes more time?

The time it takes to complete real estate classes will depend on the student. If you are an extremely motivated individual who can handle staring at a computer for hours, you might be able to finish online courses faster. If you are not motivated to take online classes, it may be faster to take in-person classes that have a set schedule. My wife went to school full-time for her license and finished in about 6 weeks. One of my team members took his classes online, and it took him about 6 months, but he also had a full-time job and a family. If you want to get your license quickly, attending in-person classes is probably the way to go.

I mentioned earlier that an agent's goals will determine their best educational path. If you want to jump in with both feet and make a career out of real estate, take an in-person class. The exposure to people in the business will be worth it. You may even have a better chance of finding the right broker once you get your license.

If you want to be a part-time agent that only uses their license for their own investments, taking online classes might make sense. You may not need the connections and personal help a real teacher will provide. However, do not expect online classes to give you guidance on getting deals.

CHAPTER 9

Do Real Estate Classes Teach You How to Sell Houses?

Many people assume real estate classes teach you how to sell houses since that is most agents' main goal. However, you'll learn much more about laws and regulations than how to sell houses. If you want to become an agent, do not depend on the licensing classes to teach you how to sell houses.

Why don't they teach you how to sell houses?

Agents choose a career in real estate to sell houses and make money. However, real estate regulatory agencies are more concerned with teaching agents the law than they are with teaching them how to make money. The real estate education system was put in place to protect consumers and make sure agents abide by the rules and regulations.

Real estate classes teach you how to stay out of trouble by driving home the legal aspects of real estate. You'll learn about contracts, appraisals, earnest money, and handling the transaction, but you won't learn how to attract buyers and sellers.

Many real estate agents learn how to sell houses from working with the right broker, but many agents do not pick the right broker. Brokerages and the amount they charge agents vary greatly. Many new agents, when choosing a broker, look at how much money they are being charged or what percentage of their commission they get to keep. The most important thing to consider when choosing a broker is how they can help you sell houses.

The brokers that charge the least usually offer the least amount of training and guidance. If you are an experienced agent who knows how to generate leads, maintain a database, and market and create your own business, maybe the least expensive brokers will work for you. But, if you are new and do not know how to sell houses, you need as much guidance as possible. If you don't sell any houses, it doesn't matter how much of your commission you keep. The best brokers will not only offer training and guidance, but also leads through floor time, advertising, and other sources.

There are many things a new agent can do, but here are the most important steps for any new agent:

- Try to take licensing classes in person so you can start networking ASAP.
- Start networking and reaching out to your circle of influence...even before you get your license.
- Choose the broker with the best training and lead sources, not the highest commission split.
- Don't be afraid to talk to successful agents in your office or area and ask them for any advice and tips.
- Talk to as many people as you can, and don't be afraid to look like an idiot at first. You must learn at some point, and the sooner you learn, the better. The best way to learn how to talk to buyers and sellers is to actually do it. Many agents get stuck in their office researching lead sources or take as many classes as they can instead of trying to meet people and sell houses.

The sooner you have a plan and a great broker to work with, and the sooner you start talking to people, the better off you will be!

CHAPTER 10

Should Prospective Agents Go to College?

Young people can be successful agents, but people ask me if potential agents should go to college first. That is a very tricky question because the answer varies for different people. I went to college and then became an agent, but I did not use much of what I learned to sell houses. However, I am glad I went to college because I learned a great deal about business. I also met a lot of great people, and it helped me mature. If I had not gone to college, I probably would not be as successful as I am now, but I also did not know whether I wanted to be an agent or not. In fact, at that point in my life I knew I did not want to be a Realtor!

Why did I go to college, and what was my major?

Both my parents went to college, and my dad graduated with a chemistry degree. My sister, who is ten years older than I, went to college and earned a doctorate in physics. My family expected me to go to college and get a degree in something. In fact, skipping college never even crossed my mind. I was always good at math, but I was by no means a straight-A student. I did not have the greatest attention span, and I had a few embarrassing moments in class when I woke up from a daydream realizing the teacher was repeatedly calling my name, waiting for an answer to some unknown question.

Because I was good at math, I thought civil engineering would be a good fit for me. I was accepted to the University of Colorado, and thoroughly hated civil engineering from the start. I realized that I was really good at basic math and numbers, but I was not good at high-level math like calculus, or at least I did not have the attention span to learn it. My freshman year, I decided that I did not want to spend the rest of my life doing high-level math problems and transferred to business school.

I chose an emphasis in finance because I liked money. After civil engineering, business school was a breeze. I took summer classes to catch up after changing majors and graduated in four years.

What did business finance teach me?

Most of business school taught the common path to success: get a corporate job, save your money, invest it in the stock market, and retire when you are 65. If you wanted to be a cut above the rest, you could work 80 hours per week, climb the corporate ladder, and hope to become a CEO or high-level corporate officer making big money. The catch was you still had to work 80 hours per week after rising to the top!

That didn't make a lot of sense to me because the chances of making it big seemed so small and the rewards required too much sacrifice. Then I took an entrepreneur class and I loved it! During that class, I worked in a group of five people, and we had to simulate running a company through a computer simulation. I took over the simulation and made all the decisions for our team, including manufacturing, budget, and marketing. I loved it, and I did not care that I was doing all the work because our team was number one in the class by a mile most of the year.

In the end, we finished third because the simulation had a flaw. In the simulation, if a company sold all its inventory, all its land, and all of its manufacturing facilities, the stock value skyrocketed. The company was basically crippled because all its assets and facilities were gone, but because the sale of those items resulted in a huge influx of cash, the stock price rose to 10 times the cash value. I explained to the teacher's assistant why a company with no possible way to make money in the future should not have a stock value so high, but she did not understand. Though I was disappointed we didn't take first, I knew I loved running a business...and I was good at it.

After college, I still did not know exactly what I wanted to do. I could not find a company that would let me be their CEO right off the bat, and I did not have any ideas for starting a business. While I figured out what I should do, I moved back to my home town and worked part-time with my dad in real estate.

I got my real estate license, helped him flip houses, and 15 years later, I am sure glad I made that choice.

I did not find immediate success, however. In the beginning, I treated it as a job and put in the hours without thinking much about what I was doing and why. I started to think about being an agent as a business. I planned my work and set goals, and my career took off. Once I started to treat it as a business, I started using my contacts from college and hired my college roommate to be my team manager.

Although college did not directly teach me how to be a real estate agent, it helped me be successful in many ways.

- I learned a lot about business and investing.
- I learned how little I wanted to be in the corporate world.
- I met a lot of very smart people and made many lifelong connections.
- I matured a lot before I started my career.
- As an alumnus, I have more contacts and better ability to network with others.

As a prospective agent, is college right for you?

College is a big life decision, and I cannot make it for you. In order to make a decision like this, write out all your options, including the pros, cons, and costs. Writing things down will make the decision much easier because you can see the benefits and downfalls. Here are things to consider:

- **Do you love real estate and do you have any experience in it?** If you have never been in the industry or around a real estate office, you may not like it. Not everyone is cut out to be an agent, and some people may enjoy the corporate world or something else much more.
- **How much will each option cost?** College is very expensive. I was lucky because my parents helped me pay for school, and I went to an in-state college with lower tuition. Tuition was also much lower then than it is now. Real estate school is much

cheaper, and in most cases, much faster to complete.

- **What are your state's licensing requirements?** Some states require a college degree, and some are considering making a degree a requirement. Check your state's requirements before you decide.
- **What type of real estate agent do you want to be?** If you want to be a residential Realtor, college will not help you get a job. But if you want to be a commercial agent, a college degree is beneficial and will help you get a job.
- **How mature are you?** Self-assessment is difficult. We all think we are mature beyond our age, but most of us are delusional when we are young. Ask your parents, your family, your friends, and anyone you know to honestly assess how mature you are and if you are ready to start a career or not. If you are not ready to take a career seriously, but you start anyway, there is a good chance you will fail. You might end up blaming your lack of success on the career and not yourself. College may be a good thing for those that need more time (I did).

After you have answered these questions, you may or may not start to get a clear idea of what is best for your situation. If you still do not know what to do, there is another option.

Can you start a real estate career while attending college?

College and a real estate career don't need to be mutually exclusive. You can choose a hybrid option. Many colleges have a real estate program or offer at least some real estate classes. You can enroll in college and choose to minor in real estate (most colleges don't offer a major in real estate), or at least take real estate classes for your electives. I recommend choosing something business related for your major because the accounting, economics, and entrepreneurial classes will be very beneficial.

Besides taking real estate classes, you could also start looking for internships or part-time jobs. Look for real estate offices who may need front-desk (or any other) kind of help. Start learning the business from people in the business. This is also a great opportunity to determine if you like the business. If you find the right company, they might help you get your license, and you may even decide you don't need your degree. Or, you might work all through college earning extra money and gaining experience. You might also realize you hate real estate and decide to pursue a different career.

There is no right answer. I am glad I went to college, but I also did not know what I wanted to do after high school. If you know you want to be an agent and nothing else, you may not need to attend college. Perhaps you can spend a year getting your license and working in a real estate office to make sure it is the right career for you. If it is the right career, you just saved a lot of money and time! If you aren't sure about real estate, or just want the college experience, try the hybrid approach, and get as involved in real estate as you can while going to school. Either way, you will have to work hard and intelligently to be successful.

CHAPTER 11

Are There Already Too Many Real Estate Agents?

A common concern among prospective agents is saturation. If there are too many agents, succeeding in real estate could become exceedingly difficult. Admittedly, there are a lot of real estate agents in the United States—over one million, in fact (as of June 2014). Despite this number, you can be successful. Even if your market is saturated, with the right attitude and plan, you too can find success.

The most successful agents sell the vast majority of houses because most agents are not very good. Many of us have dealt with subpar agents. As a Realtor myself, I constantly deal with agents who either don't know what they are doing or think just passing the real estate exam will make them successful. If you have a plan, work full-time, and have great teachers, you can make a lot of money.

Are real estate agents bad at their job?

If you have spent any time as or working with an agent, you'll know I'm not exaggerating when I say most agents are not good at their job. Many of the agents on my own team tell me they talked to buyers who were surprised when my agents answered their phone. Buyer after buyer says they call and email multiple agents with no response until they talk to our team! The only thing another agent must do to get a buyer is answer their phone, return a message, or reply to an email, yet they don't do it.

Many agents also spin their wheels chasing internet leads, chasing new marketing techniques, and chasing new clients. They forget that the core of their business is their current client base, and if they do an exceptional job for them, they will get free referrals. They see shiny objects, don't take the time to create a database, and never contact their past clients.

Why the number of agents in your market shouldn't scare you

We discussed why most agents don't sell many houses or make much money. But can you make money as a new agent? It all depends on you, your drive, your preparation, and your teachers and mentors. If a new agent concentrates on taking care of their current clients and their circle of influence, they will sell a lot of houses. You also can't be scared to tell everyone you are an agent. You provide a service and shouldn't hesitate to tell all your friends and family. Do you want your friends to use another agent when the odds say that agent may not be very good at their job? Or, do you want your friends to use you who cares deeply and will work very hard for them.

Becoming a successful agent is not about the competition; it is about you and whether you are willing to do what it takes to succeed. Most agents are not willing to do what it takes because they are worried about what people will think of them. They are too busy with new marketing techniques to answer their phone. Some people become agents because they are bored and need something to do! If you provide awesome service, remind people you are an agent, and work full-time, you will succeed.

Do not be scared off by the amount of real estate agents in your market or the average agent's income. Those numbers are very deceiving because so many agents work part-time, and many do not do what it takes to succeed. If you want to be an agent or a Realtor and are willing to do what it takes to succeed, you will.

CHAPTER 12

Can Real Estate Agents Find Success by Moving to a New Town?

One of the best ways for an agent to make money is to utilize their circle of influence. Selling houses to your friends and family is a great way to get started, especially if your friends and family refer people to you as well. However, some agents worry that they cannot be successful if they are new in town or will be moving to a new town because they have no friends or family in that town. Although having friends and family helps, you can succeed whether you have lived in a town for 30 years or you are brand new. If you only sell houses to your friends and family, you will not last very long in the business—unless you have a huge family!

What is the key to being a successful agent?

Being a successful agent is about finding clients that are likely to buy houses, doing a great job with those clients, and then reminding those clients how awesome you are. There is a lot you must do, but you don't have to have friends and family nearby to be successful. Here are some of the best ways to get clients:

- Open houses
- Advertising listings
- Building channel accounts
- Networking
- Choosing the right broker

An agent who is new to a town can accomplish each of those.

How will the right broker help an agent in a new town get business?

Possibly the most important task an agent will do is choosing the right broker. Too many agents choose brokers based on the commission split instead of on the training and support offered. Many brokers will not only offer great training but also leads from floor calls or other sources. Choosing the right broker can mean the difference between success and failure.

Open houses are a great way to get new clients. Many buyers who are not represented by a real estate agent will go to open houses. With the right techniques, a good agent should be able to get the contact information for most people who go through an open house. You don't have to have listings to hold open houses either. You should be able to find agents who will let you hold their listings open because it is free marketing for them. This is another reason to choose the right broker and office because you have a better chance of agents in your office letting you hold open houses.

Agents can also use Craigslist or other media sources to advertise listings. Any agent can advertise HUD homes, and again, you can get permission from other agents to advertise their listings.

How can building channel accounts contribute to agent success?

Channel accounts are large clients that send listings to agents over and over. Some examples of channel accounts are builders, relocation companies, and REO companies. Growing a relationship with a builder can be tough if you are new in town, but it is definitely possible. Many REO and relocation companies do not care how long you have been in town but rather how experienced you are. I know a couple of REO agents who set up shop in different areas of the country and lost very little business because of their relationships with REO companies.

The best way to build your business is by meeting people and building relationships. Building relationships in a town you know is easier, but you can also do it in a new town. Some of the best ways to get clients is to make friends with professionals who also rely on relationships to build their business. Doctors, lawyers, accountants, dentists, and many other professionals know a lot of people and talk to those people about their lives. If you can make friends with them—or better yet sell a house to them—they will tell people they know about you (as long as you do a good job!).

If you are not willing to meet new people, tell them you are a real estate agent, and build new relationships, you will not be successful in any town.

What it all comes down to is doing a great job for the clients you have. If you go above and beyond, they will tell others about you, and you will get more and more business. You can't forget to remind your past clients that you exist and are still an awesome real estate agent. Just because you may not know anyone in your town, don't be afraid of a real estate career.

CHAPTER 13

Can Young Real Estate Agents Be Successful?

I became a real estate agent when I was 22 years old. I was just out of college and did not know what to do with my life, but my father was an agent, and I decided to try the business out. It was a great decision, but success took me a few years. Some might say my youth hurt me because people don't want to work with young agents. Honestly, I do not think my age had anything to do with my success. My attitude and lack of focus prevented me from succeeding earlier, not people's perception of my abilities due to my age.

Many young readers of my blog contact me, worried that they are too young to be taken seriously. Some of these readers are much younger than I was when I first started, and I can see why they would be concerned. No one wants to begin a career where they have a huge disadvantage because no one trusts them. Although I could see a few people being concerned with using a very young agent, most people are more concerned with an agent's ability and not their age. Having the self-confidence to know what you are doing along with working for your client's best interests is much more important than how old you are. Youth also offers advantages, as some buyers and sellers may feel a younger person has a better grasp on current technology and marketing trends.

Every state has slightly different licensing requirements. Most states require you to be at least 18 years old. While you must be 18 in most states, you may be able to take both real estate classes and the test before you turn 18. Many of you may think becoming an agent at 18 is unlikely, but I have met some very ambitious youths through my blog.

How can a younger person become a successful agent?

A young person can be a great agent if they focus on the right things. The first—and possibly most important—thing to do is pick the right broker. Too many agents pick a broker that pays them the highest commission split and has the fewest costs. Unfortunately, this causes many agents to fail because they do not receive any house-selling training. I always tell people a 100 percent commission split is not a good thing if you do not sell any houses. Choose a broker that has the best training available, and if possible, has a mentoring program.

When I was young, I thought I could do everything myself and didn't need anyone to teach me how to be successful. This was one of the biggest mistakes I made because no matter what you do, there is going to be someone who has already done it and was already successful. Learn from those who have already succeeded. It will reduce the learning curve and make you more successful much sooner. My team has sold over 500 houses in the last three years. I still learn how to do things better and become more successful from real estate conferences and other agents. I also belong to coaching programs that keep me accountable and motivated.

Having goals and focus is also extremely important. Whether you are young or old, you need goals to show you where you want to be and to be able to plan the route that will get you there. When I was younger, I never set goals, and that hurt my business a lot. Once I started creating goals, my career took off. I also tried to be successful at multiple businesses at the same time. This "scatter-brained" approach helped me become mediocre at many things. No one wants a mediocre agent who is also mediocre at five other things. They want an agent who is awesome at selling houses. Focus on being the best agent you can be, and once you become an expert and set up your business, you can branch out to other businesses.

Will people take a young agent seriously?

I get asked this question all the time! People want to become real estate agents or even real estate investors, but they don't think anyone will take them seriously if they are in their teens or early twenties. Some people may be put off by a young agent, but for the most part, I don't think it will affect your business unless you let it. Most people who have bought or sold a house know many agents are not very good. They don't answer their phone; they don't return calls; and they don't follow up. If you can take care of your clients and simply return phone calls, you will be better than most agents.

Most people look for an agent who is competent, will communicate well, and knows what they are doing. Agents can demonstrate all of these qualities early on, and from that point forward, people won't care how old you are. They may even be impressed that someone so young is so ambitious.

The biggest problem a young agent will have is believing their youth will be a problem. Our mindset has a huge impact on how successful we are, and if you believe no one wants to work with you because you are young, you might subconsciously make that happen. Believe in yourself and your abilities, and people will overlook the age factor.

What are the advantages of being a young real estate agent?

If you are a young agent, many advantages outweigh the disadvantages.

- **Getting started young:** The sooner you get started at anything, the better off you will be. There is no substitute for experience and learning by doing. The longer you are in the business, the more clients and connections you will gain, which will make you more money. There is also a huge advantage to investing in real estate when you are young, and being an agent gives you an advantage as an investor.
- **Technology**: Many people believe that younger adults are better with technology. Whether this is true or not, young agents can use it to their advantage. Use technology to get more clients and

market yourself as being on top of the latest marketing trends.

- **Influence your friends**: The sooner you start investing, the better. If you are young, you probably have young friends. While many of your friends may not be ready to buy houses or invest, you can show them the benefits of rentals. Not only might you sell some houses, but you can help your friends create a better future for themselves.

- **Better to find out sooner rather than later**: What happens if you become an agent at 18, work in the business a year or two, and hate it? You are better off learning you don't like the business at 20 than figuring it out at 25 or 30. The sooner you start the business, the more time you have to figure something else out if you don't like it.

- **More time**: Often, the younger you are, the more time you have to dedicate to work. The older you get, the more responsibilities you have with family, friends and life in general. As a young agent, you have more time to commit to your clients and can therefore do a better job than many older agents who don't have any extra time.

Being a young agent does not have to be a disadvantage. Some clients may look at your youth and assume you don't know what you are doing. However, if you are confident and competent, you can show them you know what you are doing, and they may not see age as an issue. The biggest problems are only problems if you believe they are, and that affects your confidence and how you interact with people.

CHAPTER 14

Can Part-Time Real Estate Agents Successfully Sell Houses?

A lot of people have dreams of making it big in real estate, but they want to start slowly. People want the freedom, income, and other perks of being an agent but are scared to lose a steady income. Getting a real estate license and working as an agent part-time seems like a great idea, but it's more difficult to succeed if you only work part time.

On the other hand, real estate investors can work part time with much success. I own 16 long-term rentals, and I complete 10 to 15 fix-and-flips per year. I save money both when I buy a house off the MLS and whenever I sell a house because I don't have to pay a listing agent. Being a part-time agent who only uses their license for their own investing strategies might work. There are also a couple of other instances, if you have a very flexible schedule, where being a part-time agent can work. The problem with working part-time is clients need things done at all times of the day. If you can't get away from your job, you are going to find yourself struggling.

Becoming an agent takes a lot of work

One of the drawbacks of becoming a part-time real estate agent is how much work it takes to become one. It can take hundreds of hours of education and testing. If you already have a job, even part-time, finding time to complete the education will be tough.

You can take night or online classes, but you are going to have to spend a lot of time studying. The real estate exam is not easy to pass, and preparing for it takes a long time. If you want to become a part-time agent, make sure you factor in the time it will take to get your license.

Once you get your license, you must hang it with a broker. After finding a brokerage, you must start working with clients and generating business. This is where it gets tricky for a part-time agent who may have another full-time or part-time job. Whether you are listing houses or working with buyers, selling real estate is a random-hours job. You may not have to work 40 hours per week, but you do have to work all hours of the day.

If you have a full- or part-time job during the day, you better be able to get away from that job to take real estate calls. Buyers are going to want to look at houses, and offers will need to be negotiated and presented. If your clients have to wait 8 hours to get a hold of you, they are going to get frustrated. If you don't get back to your clients in a timely manner, there is a good chance you will lose them. In a tight seller's market like we have now, speed is very important in getting offers accepted. If buyers feel an agent can't submit offers fast enough, they will probably find another agent.

Most people think being an agent is about showing houses and writing offers. There is much more to it than that, and that is why we get paid so much for selling houses. Agents must do many things to close deals and generate business. Here are some of the things an agent must do to be successful:

- Show houses
- Write contracts
- Help buyers complete inspections
- Contact lenders
- Contact title companies
- Contact other agents
- Complete continuing education
- Hold open houses
- Talk to their circle of influence
- Create brochures
- Take pictures
- Create advertisements
- Answer their phone
- Floor duty
- Create plans and goals
- Manage their expenses

As you can see, a successful agent has many responsibilities. Not only do you have to work with clients, but you also must find them. Being a great agent takes significant time and energy, and it's very difficult to do part time. Being able to answer your phone at any time is one of the best ways to get business. If you are returning calls hours after you receive them, you risk losing your clients to another agent who returns calls quickly.

Can part-time agents maintain a good reputation?

I deal with a lot of other agents, title companies, buyers, and sellers. I also deal with lenders, attorneys, investors, and many different people in our community. My reputation is a huge reason why I sell a lot of houses every year. When you are a part-time agent, finding enough time for tasks and follow-up is very difficult. If you don't return calls for days—or not at all—word will spread around the real estate community very quickly. Providing great service is key, but it is tough to do when you only work part time.

If you earn a reputation as someone who is hard to reach, doesn't call back, or is too busy to follow up, you will have a hard time changing your image. Even if you become a full-time agent, and do an amazing job, people will remember your subpar work. People remember poor work and expect people to do good work.

If you want to be a part-time agent, join a team.

If you want to be a part-time agent and there is no possible way you can quit your current job, there are some steps you can take to be more successful. My team has part-time help, and many members of my team started out as part-time workers. If you join a team, they can help cover for you when you must work your other job. By joining a team, you agree to give up part of your commission to the team, so the team is motivated to help you succeed. You have a much better chance of succeeding as a part-time agent if you can join a team instead of trying to do it all yourself.

How else can part-time agents succeed?

Besides joining a team, you have other options to make your part-time real estate career work. Most importantly, you must be available. Many people do not want to be on-call all the time, but you must make sacrifices if you want an awesome career. While you may not have to work 30 hours or even 20 hours per week to sell houses, you need to be available most of the time. If a buyer or seller needs to talk to you on a Sunday afternoon or a Monday morning, you should be available. You may have to show houses on the weekends or in the evenings. Agents make their own schedules and have a lot of freedom, but when a client needs to see a house after hours, the agent should accommodate them.

If you want to be a part-time agent and have a very flexible schedule, you have a much better chance of making it. If you have to work another 9 to 5 job every day, it will be very tough to make a real estate career work.

Conclusion

A part-time agent can make it in the real estate industry, but to be successful, part-timers need to join a team or have a flexible schedule until they can go full-time. If you are an investor who just wants to save money on their own investment properties, becoming a part-time agent is a great idea.

Many of my sales come from listing REO and HUD homes for banks and the government. If you ever want to become an REO agent, you must work at it full time. Banks and HUD will need responses right away, and getting back to them in a day or two won't cut it. I must do inspections in 24 hours or less on many of my properties, or I'll get fired.

PART III

CHAPTER 15

What Can You Do to Build Your Business before You Become a Real Estate Agent?

Getting a real estate license can be difficult for some and easy for others. Some people are great test takers, and some states have fewer requirements than others. There is much more to becoming an agent than just getting a license. You should start learning how to sell houses and build a business well before you ever get your license or start taking classes.

The first thing anyone should do before they start a new career is set goals and plan what they want out of life. Planning and setting goals will help you determine if real estate is the right career choice.

Your career choice should not be taken lightly. Success doesn't come easy, and the hard work begins as soon as you have an inkling that you want to begin. Not only will planning and setting goals help you determine whether to become an agent, it will also help you be more successful because you will have a clear direction. Don't be afraid to set big goals!

After you have set goals and decided that you want to be an agent, it is time to take action. You might think step one is signing up for real estate classes, but before you sign up, start telling people you are becoming an agent. The most important thing you can do is build your circle of influence. The more people you know and the more referrals you get, the more money you will make. Whether it takes one or four months to get your license, you can use that time to start spreading the word. The sooner you start building up business, the sooner you will make money.

What is the best way to get your real estate license?

Even though I took my classes online, it is best to take classes in person if you want to work in real estate full time. I already talked about how important it is to network, and real estate classes are a great way to network. In-person classes will have an experienced teacher, other like-minded students, and guest speakers, all of who can help your business one way or another.

If you are interested in taking online classes, Real Estate Express is the company most of the agents on my team used to get their license.

How do you choose a broker?

Well before you obtain your license, you should also determine which office and broker you want to work with. Every new agent must work under a broker. A good broker can help a real estate agent succeed...quickly. If a broker does not have much interest in helping their agents, it will be tough for a new agent to succeed and learn the business. Every office also has a different commission and fee structure, and it is best to research this information before you get your license.

Don't be afraid to ask others in the real estate business for help

I have a habit of trying to do everything myself without asking for help. I have worked hard to change this habit and ask for help when I can because the more help I have, the more successful I will be. Do not shy away from calling successful agents in your area and taking them to lunch. Learn the secrets to their success and listen to their advice. Those agents may also know which offices are the best in your area. Some successful agents may even be looking for help on their team and may have a job for you. Starting with a team is much easier and cheaper than going it alone.

Remember, this career should not be taken lightly. I know many agents who took real estate classes online, got their license, and then had no idea what do to. They had not researched offices, and some had no idea what it took to be an agent. The more research and planning you can do, the more successful you will be. Set goals, plan your future, and set yourself up for success well before you get your license.

CHAPTER 16

Why Must Real Estate Agents Work Under a Broker?

Many people assume that once they get their license, they can start selling houses right away. Yet in almost every state, new agents must work under a broker, which doesn't mean you have to work on their team or be an assistant—it means you must "hang" your license in the office of a broker.

Each state has different classifications for what they call agents and brokers. In Colorado, any agent who does not have their employing broker's or independent broker's license is called a Broker Associate. Some states use the word "agents," and other states use different wording for each classification. I will use the term agent, which will mean anyone with a real estate license who is not a broker in charge of their own office.

The broker where a new agent hangs their license is usually called a managing or employing broker and oversees all the agents in their office. I don't know of any states that let new agents oversee themselves. The managing broker is responsible for every agent in their office and every agent's actions.

In Colorado, an agent must hang their license in a managing broker's office for at least two years before they are eligible to go out on their own as a broker. Each broker requires different responsibilities and fees from their agents.

What rules do brokers set for agents?

Every broker and every office will have slightly different rules for their agents. It is up to the broker to come up with the rules and determine how little or how much the agent needs to be involved in the office. Some large brokerages will require training, a certain amount of hours calling people, open houses, and other tasks. Those large offices may also offer the agent leads, a mentor, office space, a secretary, and other services. Other offices will require nothing from the agent and in turn won't offer the agent any services.

The amount brokers charge varies widely depending on what the broker offers. In offices where the agent has a physical desk and a secretary, the fees can be very high. Our office has about 35 agents. We always have at least one staff person answering the phones. We also have an office manager and about 12 offices for agents. Additionally, we offer community offices that agents who work at home can use when they visit. It costs $500 per month to have your own private office, but if you work at home, you don't pay a desk fee. Agents also have to pay a portion of their commissions to our broker. We have a number of different packages, ranging from 50/50 commission splits, no commission splits, and base fee paid by the agent to the broker every year. Not only does our broker provide staff and office space, but he also provides some supplies and advertising. He has an advertising deal with the local paper and with Homes and Land Magazine, and each agent is allowed to use a certain amount of advertising each month.

Some brokerages only have agents that work at home, and they offer no services. The agent is expected to answer all calls, complete all paperwork, do all advertising, and do everything else themselves. Those brokerages are very cheap but offer the agent very little help. Many agents go this route to avoid desk fees and large commission splits.

What is a commission split?

When an agent sells a house, they earn a commission, which is a percentage of the sale price. There isn't a standard commission in the real estate world, but we will use 3% for each side of a commission as an example. That means the listing agent who represents the seller and the selling agent who represents the buyer each gets 3% of the purchase price when the house sells. If you represent the seller on a house that sells for $200,000, the listing agent would get $6,000 (3% from the sale and 3% from the purchase). However, the commission is not paid directly to the real estate agent—it is paid to the managing broker. The broker then decides how that commission will be paid to the agent. The broker/agent agreement will determine how much money the agent takes home after the broker gets their cut.

Some brokerages will offer new agents a 50/50 commission split because those agents need a lot of training, help, and guidance. Brokerages may offer a sliding scale for the number of houses you sell in a year. If an agent sells 50 houses, they get a 90/10 split; if they sell 25, they get a 75/25 split, and so on. Some brokerages may vary the splits based on the agent's client. If the agent uses a client referred by the broker, they may only earn 30% of the commission, but if the agent sells to one of their own clients, they may earn 80% of the commission.

Commission-split structures vary widely, and some no-service brokerages will offer 100% commission splits to the agents and only charge base monthly fees. Again, these companies do not offer any services, and the agent is pretty much on their own to figure everything out.

What would I suggest for new agents?

This is tricky because everyone has different goals and different reasons for getting their real estate license. For people who want to be full-time agents and make real estate their career, I highly suggest choosing an office with a mentor and training program. That training and experience will more than make up for the extra costs and lower commission splits. The ideal situation may be to join a successful agent or broker's team who will pay you as an assistant while you learn from them. If you are an investor who only wants to use your license for your own deals, you may not want to be in a time-consuming training program.

I would look for an office that offers high commission splits with no hourly requirements but still offers training. As a new agent, you are going to need some training and guidance, even if you only work your own deals. Figuring out all the paperwork and requirements on your own is difficult. I would stay away from no-service brokerages until you have a solid idea of what you are doing and know the basics.

What will brokers help with?

An agent must find someone who can train them and teach them how to be a good agent. Here are some of the things an agent must learn. I cannot teach this in a book because every market is different, and agents need to be trained locally on many of these tasks.

- **How to value a house**: One of the most important things an agent can do is value houses correctly. Price a house too high, and it costs the seller money. Price it too low, and it costs the seller money. Give an investor the wrong value on a fixed-up house, and they can lose money on a deal.
- **How to find houses for sale:** Most agents use the MLS to find listings for buyers. Different MLS systems, use different terms and can be searched in different ways. You need to be an expert at using your local MLS system. Most MLS systems offer alerts to email clients new listings. You need to know how to set up these alerts.
- **Know what is customary in your area:** Different areas of the country have different processes. Some states use attorneys to close houses and others use title companies. In some areas, houses must have washers and dryers to be salable, and in others, they are almost never included. In some areas, a pool is very valuable and in others, it decreases the value.
- **Know what marketing works in your area:** Different marketing techniques work better in different areas and different neighborhoods. A mentor can help you determine what marketing to use and how to use it.
- **Learn how to use contracts:** Each state has a different sales contract and rules for agents. The broker can help new agents learn how to write and use contracts to help their clients get the best deal.

Obviously, an agent must have a lot of knowledge. It is not all about selling houses and finding clients. A broker can help you find clients and make sure you do things right. It is very tough for a new agent to learn this all on their own.

CHAPTER 17

How Can You Find the Perfect Broker to Work With?

The type of broker a new real estate agent will want to work with will depend on that agent's needs and goals. An investor who only wants to get a license to help them buy their own houses will not need the same type of broker as an agent looking to make a career out of real estate. Finding the perfect broker for your needs isn't easy, but it is extremely important.

Every new agent has different goals and aspirations. Those goals will determine what type of broker will work best. An agent who is looking to start a career in real estate will want a broker that will offer training and accountability. The agent might make less money on each deal with a higher commission split going to the broker, but they will probably sell many more houses and make more money. Plus, they'll get training and will be held accountable. Many new agents will choose a brokerage based on the best split they can get, but selling real estate without help isn't easy. If you don't sell any houses, the commission split your broker offers is irrelevant.

If an agent either has a team or is planning to create a team, they should ask potential brokers how they structure teams. Some offices are very team-friendly and others are not.

Once you decide what type of broker you want to work with, you must find them. I recommend working with brokers that are selling the most houses. If a brokerage sells many houses, the community will recognize the company name. Buyers and sellers want to make sure the agent or company they are working with is successful and knows what they are doing. Even if an agent is brand new and has never sold a house, the company they work for may have a great reputation for selling houses, and the buyers or sellers will assume that agent does as well. Another advantage of offices that sell many houses is they might provide their agents with leads. Some offices offer floor time or open-house opportunities, which can be a huge boost to a new agent's business.

To find the offices of brokers that do the most business, look on Zillow or another house-listing site. Look for offices that list the most houses in your area, and start calling them. Most brokers are actively looking for new agents and will be excited to talk to you.

You should be able to set up a meeting with a couple of brokers to see if they are a good fit. If they aren't what you are looking for, ask the broker which office they would suggest working with. Don't be shy. Ask for help or suggestions. If you are having trouble finding brokers, try these techniques:

- Ask friends and family which real estate offices they have worked with.
- Check Facebook for real estate agent or office posts; they are all over the place!
- Do a simple web search for real estate in your area. Many offices will pop up.
- Ask title companies or lenders which agents or offices they work with.
- Ask your real estate school for recommendations.

After enough calls and meetings, you should be able to find a few brokers to meet with.

What should you ask a potential real estate broker?

When you start vetting brokers, you need to know what questions to ask. Before you ask these questions, you should consider what you want the answer to be.

- What commission splits do they offer? This can vary from 50/50 or less, to 100% with a transaction fee. Commission splits can also vary based on how much business they do.
- What services do they offer their agents? Do they offer administrative assistants, a showing service to set up appointments on their listings, and advertising? Do they pay for signs? Do they have a website for their agents, email addresses, office

space, phone service, printers and paper, and computers?

- Do they charge buyers or sellers a transaction fee on top of the commission? Some offices do this, and it is a surprise to the clients, meaning the agent sometimes pays it.
- Do they offer lead-generation for the agents? Is floor time available? Does the office work with Zillow or another lead generation source? How do they determine who gets leads and floor time?
- How much office time is an agent expected to put in? Is there an at-home or part-time agent option (not suggested)?
- What kind of training does the real estate broker offer? Do they offer mentors, accountability, courses, or other training, and is it mandatory?
- How many agents are in the office, and is the office losing or gaining agents?

I cannot give you the answers to these questions. However, I can tell you it is much more important to choose a broker with the best training rather than the broker with the lowest fees. It is much better to sell 20 houses your first year and pay 50 percent of your commission to the broker than to sell 1 house in your first year and pay only 10 percent to your broker.

What if you choose the wrong broker?

If you are already working with a broker you do not like or chose a broker that is a bad fit, move! The longer you stay with a broker that doesn't fit you, the worse off you will be. Depending on the broker, you may lose some listings or some deals you have under contract, but you need to move to a broker that fits you. The longer you stay with a broker who does not help you sell houses, the more money it will cost you. Don't think you made a bad choice; it may not even be your fault. Some brokers promise everything they can to get new agents but do not deliver on their promise.

One of the agents on our team was looking at a different broker when he first got his license. The broker promised him leads and a spot on his team. The agent went through the education and passed the real estate test. When he contacted that broker again, the broker barely remembered who he was and said there was no room on his team and no one in the office to mentor him. The agent was obviously very confused and a bit shocked. Lucky for my team, he did some searching and joined us. In his first year, he made over $100,000. I think he is pretty happy the broker forgot about the promises he made.

CHAPTER 18

What Is the Difference Between a Realtor and a Real Estate Agent?

Many people think real estate agents and Realtors are the same thing. However, there are some big differences. If you are a buyer or seller, a Realtor will have different and more ethical responsibilities than an agent, but does that really make a difference to a buyer or seller? I was a Realtor for 14 years, but I recently became an agent only.

Why would an agent want to be a Realtor?

Being an agent involves getting licensed in the state you want to work in and hanging your license with a broker. As of March 25, 2016, there were 1,150,141 Realtors in the United States out of about 2,500,000 real estate agents. About half of all agents are Realtors. Being a Realtor comes with many perks besides just being able to say you are one. Many MLS boards require their members be a Realtor to gain access to the MLS, or the boards charge more to those who are not Realtors.

Being a Realtor also gives you access to many organizations:

- **NAR:** National Association of Realtors.
- **State Board of Realtors:** Most states have a state board of Realtors.
- **Local Board of Realtors:** Most areas have a local board of Realtors specific to your market location.

I work in Northern Colorado and once belonged to CAR (Colorado Association of Realtors) and GARA (Greeley Area Realtor Association). When I was a member of those boards, I could attend local meetings, luncheons, classes, and charity events put on by those boards. I could also run for leadership roles.

How much does becoming a Realtor cost?

One drawback to becoming a Realtor is it is more expensive than becoming an agent. Here are the fees I pay for various boards. These will vary based on your specific board and your state:

- NAR: $120 per year
- NAR: $35 special assessment per year
- CAR: $165 per year
- GARA: $209.17 per year
- **Total: $519.17**

These fees are separate from any MLS dues and fees that must be paid. As you can see, being a Realtor is expensive, and I also pay for the agents on my team to be Realtors, so it costs me thousands of dollars per year. This is one reason I am no longer a Realtor.

Why would buyers and sellers prefer to work with a Realtor?

Realtors are also supposed to be held to a higher level of ethics.

Below are the pledges a Realtor makes. Agents are not required to make these pledges:

- Pledge to put the interests of buyers and sellers ahead of their own and to treat all parties honestly.
- Shall refrain from exaggerating, misrepresenting, or concealing material facts; and is obligated to investigate and disclose when situations reasonably warrant.
- Shall cooperate with other brokers/agents when it is in the best interests of the client to do so.
- Have a duty to disclose if they represent family members who own or are about to buy real estate, or if they themselves are a principal in a real estate transaction, that they are licensed to sell real estate.
- Shall not provide professional services in a transaction where the agent has a present or contemplated interest without disclosing that interest.

- Shall not collect any commissions without the seller's knowledge nor accept fees from a third-party without the seller's express consent.
- Shall refuse fees from more than one party without all parties' informed consent.
- Shall not co-mingle client funds with their own.
- Shall attempt to ensure that all written documents are easy to understand and will give everybody a copy of what they sign.
- Shall not discriminate in any fashion for any reason on the basis of race, color, religion, sex, handicap, familial status, or national origin.
- Expects agents to be competent, to conform to standards of practice, and to refuse to provide services for which they are unqualified.
- Must engage in truth in advertising.
- Shall not practice law unless they are a lawyer.
- Shall cooperate if charges are brought against them and present all evidence requested.
- Agree not to bad mouth competition and agree not to file unfounded ethics complaints.
- Shall not solicit another REALTOR'S client nor interfere in a contractual relationship.
- Shall submit to arbitration to settle matters and not seek legal remedies in the judicial system.

Realtors market themselves as abiding by these standards, where real estate agents may not have to abide by them (depending on state laws). In my experience, many Realtors and agents practice unethically. Personally, I haven't noticed an ethical difference between Realtors and agents. When we have had problems with unethical Realtors, the boards did not do much to help us out.

While Realtors can advertise that they are held to a higher level than just agents, I do not think it makes much difference to a buyer or seller.

Why did I stop being a Realtor?

I was a Realtor for almost 15 years, but last year (2016), I dropped my membership. It was costing me thousands of dollars per year with few benefits. Most buyers and sellers do not care if I am a Realtor, and I had a few problems with how NAR handled some issues. My primary business is listing foreclosures for banks. I worked hard, for years, to build my business with banks and REO companies. I reached the point where I was selling 200 houses per year. A few years ago, NAR decided that REO brokers like myself had too much business and that every agent should be able list REO homes without putting the work in. NAR lobbied to force banks and REO companies to include more agents and take business away from existing agents. That did not sit well with me. Plus, I've found a few other decisions they have made to be questionable.

Conclusion

Becoming a real estate agent is not cheap. Getting your license and insurance takes money, and you may have to pay part of your commissions to a broker. Becoming a Realtor is even more expensive, and I do not see a huge advantage to it.

CHAPTER 19

How Do Real Estate Agents Sell Houses?

This is the chapter many of you have been waiting for! What can agents do to make money and bring in clients? There are many ways to get clients, and some are easier than others. I love REO and having listings come in with little work involved. Now, it took a ton of work to establish my REO accounts, and I still work to bring in new accounts, but the payoff was fantastic. I say "was" because REO listings have virtually vanished in Colorado due to the increase in market prices. REO can be a great business when the market is down, but you cannot rely on REO when the market is strong. That is why I built a team that can handle a high number of REO properties when foreclosures are numerous and a team of agents who are great at selling traditional houses when foreclosures are scarce.

I have 6 licensed agents, and they do a great job of making me money. I also have started moving towards more retail sales now that REO sales have dwindled. The great part about real estate is there are so many ways to make money. If one way of making money isn't working, try something else. If you don't like working with buyers, work with sellers.

How to increase income as a buyer's agent

Buyer's agents are limited by the amount of time they have in the day, but they can still make good money. My father worked primarily with buyers for over 30 years and was very successful, selling over 100 houses over multiple years. The first thing a buyer's agent must do is get leads. There are many ways to get leads, and some are better than others.

Circle of influence

The easiest and best way to start getting clients is to tell everyone you know. You need to tell people you are getting your license, and tell them again once you have your license. Then, you have to continue to remind them. Your friends and family will want to help you get started and will use you, even if you have no experience, so don't be afraid to promote yourself! Would you rather your friends and family use another agent who will most likely do a worse job than you...or who won't care as much? No! So, don't be afraid to market yourself.

Marketing yourself does not mean you must ask your friends if they want to buy or sell a house every time you see them. It means you put them on your marketing list and remind them you are an agent, just like you would past clients. It also means you talk about your job and how it is going. Remind them, in a subtle manner, that you're an agent...and hopefully a great one!

Open houses

Sitting in an open house will bring buyers to you, but it's not the most exciting thing in the world. Many buyers who visit open houses are not very serious, and many are already working with an agent. Whenever you meet a potential buyer or seller, always ask if they are working with an agent. The first rule in real estate is don't poach another agent's client. It is unethical. If you hold enough open houses and talk to enough people, you will find buyers. You can hold an open house wherever at any agent's listing...if they allow it. Usually, real estate agents love when other agents hold open houses since it gives their listings more exposure. A typical open house occurs for a couple of hours on the weekend. You can also hold open houses during the week. Open houses held in the afternoon can be a great way to catch people picking up their kids from school.

The key to holding a successful open house is getting a buyer's information so you can follow up with them. Open houses are not a very good way to sell a listing, but they are a great way to find buyers. Holding contests or raffles is a great way to get information. Bring a signup sheet for visitors and give away a gift card to the raffle winner. The only entry requirement is a name and phone number. Whether they win or lose, it is a great way to call them up and let them know if they won or not. You can also hold a contest to guess how many M&Ms are in a jar. You get the idea. Come up with something fun! You should also educate yourself about other listings in the area if buyers do not like the house. This gives you an opportunity to talk to the buyers and get to know them better, which is what real estate is all about.

Advertising in local papers

It may seem a bit outdated, but people do still read newspapers. Many newspapers are now online and will post classifieds both in print and online. Newspapers are a great place to advertise open houses, listings, or buyer ads. My father would always advertise to first-time buyers in the paper, and those ads brought him a lot of business. Newspaper advertisements can be very expensive but effective if used right.

You can advertise individual listings, which will get you buyer leads and make your sellers happy. You can advertise special lending programs in your area. You can advertise other agent's listings, with their permission. Advertising in big papers will give you a bigger audience, but do not ignore smaller papers. Smaller papers will have fewer readers but also less competition from other agents.

House magazines

Almost every area in the country has a magazine dedicated to houses for sale. Homes and Land is our main local house-for-sale magazine. It is free and readily available in most public places. This is another listings or buyer-advertising outlet. House magazines can be very effective because people pick them up when eating or waiting in a doctor's office. Many people will browse a house magazine before they will pick up a newspaper. We have advertised in Homes and Land for years.

Online advertising through real estate sites

Online advertising is the big thing now. Because I'm an agent, online companies call me weekly, trying to sell me advertising. We are in the process of trying out different online advertising outlets. Right now, we use Zillow, which advertises our picture and information next to listings on their site.

We formerly used Trulia, but we stopped due to poor-quality leads. I think many online sites focus on getting anyone to ask for more information so they can sell those leads. That, in turn, produces very low-quality leads. Zillow is a little better than Trulia, but closing a deal still requires numerous online leads. Online leads tend to be disloyal because the potential buyers have no idea who you are.

Your own website

Every real estate agent should have their own website that advertises their services and listings. If you have no idea how to do this, hire someone (like I did). The person I hired happens to be on my team, but many companies exist that will build websites for agents. Make sure your website works and is easy to navigate. You don't want to turn off potential clients by sending them to a page that does not work.

You should include a personal bio and your company description, and you should advertise your listings and services. You can also set up your web page to search MLS listings right from your website (IDX). Having an MLS function on your website is nice but not necessary. We focus on who we are and what our team is good at. I think most agents have MLS feeds on their website, but few people use those feeds. Consumers are more likely to use Zillow or another site to look at listings. Our website constantly brings in leads. We use Facebook and Google AdWords to market the page, and unlike Zillow, the leads we get from our own website are very high quality.

The ultimate goal is to attract people searching for houses in your area to your site. The best way to do this, besides have listings, is to post blog articles. Successful blogs should contain eight articles per month. The articles should be at least 750 words long, contain pictures and useful information about how to buy houses, and provide market conditions or other local information that people may search for. If you take the time to write articles, make sure you post them on Facebook or Twitter, and send them to your email list!

Use for-sale signs and listings to obtain buyer leads

You may have noticed a common trend: listings bring in buyers. No matter how great your advertising is, nothing beats attractively priced listings. Listing houses is the best way to make a lot of money in real estate, and listing will help you eventually start a team. REO homes are usually very attractively priced and will bring in even more buyers.

When you list a house, you put up a for-sale sign containing your name and number. This is an awesome way to advertise, especially if you have nice color brochures in the flyer box. The other interesting thing about listings is big real estate sites will automatically add listings from the MLS. Zillow, homes.com, realtor.com, trulia.com, and more all advertise my listings for free!

Having listings allows you to do more open houses, advertise more, and have more material for your website.

Mailing campaigns

One way to get listings is to canvas neighborhoods. Canvassing means choosing a neighborhood and targeting it with multiple mailings or door hangers. The more consistent mailers someone receives, the better the chance they'll remember your name. There are many ways to send out mailers, including just-sold cards, house-values pamphlets, or even recipes or sports-team schedules. Providing something of interest or something people will keep is the key. You must continue to send things or people will think you stopped selling real estate.

The most important and profitable mail campaign includes your past and current clients and your circle of influence.

Statistics show gaining a new client is 6 times more expensive than keeping a current one. You must convince new clients you know what you are doing, that you're a hard worker, and that you are responsive and can get the job done. A past client should already know these things and will just need to be reminded you are still in the business.

You can send mailings or emails to your past-client and contacts database. Include everyone you know because the people who know you best will tell you what marketing they like best and what made the best impression. Feedback is vitally important so you know what is working and what is not.

We send one quarterly newsletter and monthly emails to all our contacts. Running a successful real estate business is not cheap: you'll have to spend money to make money. The cost of sending newsletters, canvassing neighborhoods, advertising in magazines, and paying for online advertising adds up. It can cost thousands of dollars per year or even per month, depending on how big you want to be.

One of the most important reasons to constantly communicate with your database is to have them refer you to their friends and family (and if your current contacts are looking for a house, you'll remind them that you're an agent). A house is the biggest purchase most people make, and people discuss it with their friends and family. If people don't have an agent, and you keep in constant contact, there is a great chance your contacts will recommend you.

Expired listings

Each state has rules preventing you from contacting sellers to solicit business if they already listed their home with an agent. However, once a house expires on the MLS or the listing agreement expires, you can contact those sellers. To try to pick up the listing, many agents will contact every expired and withdrawn listing they see in the MLS. I personally do not use this technique. If you call another agent's clients as soon as the listing has expired, you may annoy other agents.

That does not mean the strategy does not work, but it is not for me. I can't do everything!

Cold calling

Yes, cold calling still exists. I don't cold call or knock on doors, but it can be a successful tactic. The great part about cold calling and door knocking is it is free! If you call enough people and knock on enough doors, you will eventually get some business. However, make sure you abide by the no-call list.

Craigslist

Craigslist is another free advertising source. You can advertise to buyers or advertise your listings. There are a lot of agents on Craigslist now, and picking up business is not as easy as it used to be, but it does still work. I would put every listing you get on Craigslist. Advertise for first-time buyers and anything else you specialize in.

Facebook, LinkedIn, social media

We list all our houses on Facebook, and I have a LinkedIn page, Twitter Page, Pinterest Page, and more. These sites are all free, and there are buyers and sellers everywhere! I set up a business page on Facebook, and most of my marketing is done on the business page and not my personal page. I have seen agents use their personal page very effectively as well. If you had to pick one site to focus on, I would choose Facebook. When you set up a business page, you can post:

- New listings.
- Sold properties.
- Local events.
- Blog articles relating to real estate or the city you work in.
- News about yourself.
- Charity Events.
- Anything else that is interesting.

Facebook is tricky because not all your friends and not everyone who likes your business page will see your posts. Facebook decides how many people to send your post to based on how popular the post is. The more people who like it, share it, click on it, or comment on it, the more people will see it. Therefore, it is very important to mix things up and post interesting things. Hold contests and get people commenting if possible. There are companies that will post for you, but I have found that they seem "fake" and do not get much of a response. It is best if you can post things or hire someone to post things that are local. If someone comments on your post, make sure you reply and encourage more comments.

We also do paid advertising on Facebook. Facebook allows you to boost posts from your business page, and it is not very expensive. Not only does boosting posts get more people to see your information, it gets your pages more likes. The more likes you have, the more people you will reach. When you set up your business page, make sure you ask all your friends and family to like the page to help it get off the ground. It is also possible to buy likes, but I would not do this, as they are very low quality and most people will dislike the page after a few weeks or months.

Marketing to pre-foreclosures

Short sales still take place across the country, and many agents make a living selling only short sales. The trick to selling short sales is finding and selling them before they go to foreclosure. There are ways to get lists of homeowners in default or who have had legal filings against them. In Colorado, we can look up owners who are in foreclosure through the Public Trustee website.

If you want to focus on short sale listings, you need to send out mailers, advertise on Craigslist, or find another way to get to sellers as soon as possible. The sooner you can talk to them, the better chance you have of selling their house before it goes into foreclosure. There are many short sale courses and designations that can help you gain credibility and find leads. I am a Certified Distressed Property Expert (CDPE), which is one of the more recognized courses.

Conclusion

There are many ways to get leads, but the truth is, the best leads come from you. This consists of your friends, your family, and people you come into contact with on a regular basis. The more people you know, the more leads you will have and the more houses you will sell. The million-dollar question is how do you get to know as many people as possible and create genuine relationships? You use systems like you would with any successful business. You keep track of who you talk to, the calls you make, and the actions you take to meet people.

CHAPTER 20

Why Real Estate Agents Should Join a Team

I've covered many things an agent can do to generate income. If you are a brand-new agent, you cannot do them all, and you wouldn't want to do them all even if you could. To be successful, you need to be focused on one or two ways to make money. Once you have mastered a couple of techniques, you can add more and more. One way to drastically cut down the learning curve and learn where you should focus your time is to join a team.

Agents create teams for many reasons. Most agents' goal is to sell a lot of houses by building up their client base and getting referrals from past clients and their circle of influence. When a real estate agent builds a big enough circle of influence, they will start to earn many referrals and leads. Some agents are happy doing enough business to keep themselves busy, while others look to expand and take advantage of all those leads. When a real estate agent gets busy, their first hire should be an assistant to help with contracts and paperwork. If an agent has an assistant to help with the busy work yet still can't keep up, they hire more agents.

Agents who start a team will make money off the agents they hire because they take a split of the agents' commissions. To attract agents, some lead agents will provide training, pay office bills, and offer other perks. When an agent becomes successful, starting a team is a great way to build off their success by adding agents and making money without selling more houses themselves.

Getting started is difficult because you make money when you sell houses, and it can take months before you sell your first house. The average agent makes less than $20,000 in their first year because establishing themselves takes time. As a new agent figuring out how to get leads, what to spend money on, and how to sell houses can prove to be difficult.

When you choose a broker to work with, they may or may not offer training. Learning from a mentor who has found success in your market is the best way to learn how to sell houses and build your business. It will drastically reduce the learning curve and save you money as well.

What commission split will a real estate team offer new agents?

The lead agent will take a part of each agent's commission in return for the services and training they offer. However, that does not mean a new agent will earn much less on a team than they would on their own. New agents will usually receive a lower commission split than experienced agents. The fewer houses you sell, the less money you make the office and the smaller commission split you will receive. The team leader most likely sells a lot of houses and will have a very high commission split. In some cases, the team leader may even be the broker and will not have to split any of his team's commissions with the office. In my office, I am not the broker, but I am on a 100 percent commission split because I pay my broker a base fee every year.

Since the lead agent gets most or all the commission, they can pay agents on their team close to what that agent would make on their own. I offer agents on my team a 50/50 split on all deals. Some teams offer different commissions depending on where a lead came from, the team, or the agent. I offer the same split no matter where the lead came from because I want agents working just as hard on my leads as their own. It's also difficult to know where a lead actually came from because calls come in from for-sale signs and other sources that cannot be tracked.

Even though some teams may offer a higher split than others, an agent does not always want the higher split. New agents need training and mentoring to learn the business and become successful. The more training an agent gets, the more deals they will do, and the more money they will make. Higher commission splits do not mean more money but usually do mean less training and help.

As we've discussed, real estate courses do not teach you how to get business. You must learn how to build your business on your own or with the help of a mentor. Here are a few things a new agent will learn from a real estate team.

- Many companies out there promise great leads. Some of those lead sources are okay and some are a complete rip-off. The best way to build a business is not from buying leads but from building a database from people you already know. A real estate team will help you decide where to spend money and which programs are worth paying for.
- A great real estate team will also provide new agents with training. I hold a team meeting every week that includes training sessions, and I am thinking about holding meetings every day to increase my team's performance. My training sessions discuss lead sources, how to talk to clients, how to talk to new leads, what you can and can't say, how to prospect, how to work with investors, and much more.
- A real estate team will help agents with paperwork and contracts. My least favorite part of real estate is dealing with paperwork. Assistants on my team handle almost all paperwork for me, and they help other agents on my team with paperwork as well. We teach our agents how to handle inspections, appraisals, loans, closings, contracts, the MLS, and more, but my assistant can create all the contracts and addendums for those tasks.
- Our team teaches agents how to build a database. We teach our agents how to meet and contact people, , who to contact, and how to follow up. This is the most important part of being an agent, and new agents usually have no idea how to get started with it.

How will a real estate team help new agents make more money?

I already discussed why a lower commission split with a team may not equal less money for a new agent. How exactly can a real estate team help a new agent make more money?

- A team will help you learn the business, and in many cases, they will give you leads. I let my team put name riders on my listings, and their names go on all the advertising. I don't work with buyers because I am busy with many other money-making activities. We also have a lead line that goes to agents' cell phones in a round-robin style format. That line has leads coming in from advertising, websites, Zillow, and many more sources.

- My team makes our agents hold open houses to get business. We have many listings, which makes it easy for our agents to find houses to hold open. We also provide training on the best way to hold open houses and get clients from them.

- My goal is to have every agent on my team take home $100,000 per year. The more money my agents make, the more money I make. I am motivated to help my agents succeed and sell as many houses as possible. Not only does a team help agents sell houses by providing leads and training, but it also provides motivation and pushes agents to succeed.

- A team should provide their agents with books, CDs, and other learning material. I signed up for a real estate agent training course that provides training CDs every month. We give those CDs to all our agents, and we also give them good books to help them succeed.

- A good real estate team should hold agents accountable. We help our agents create and track their goals in the business and in life. We provide tracking sheets that help agents determine how many people they have to talk to and meet to reach those goals.

- My team holds events like happy hours that the entire team attends and invites clients to. These events help our team build better relationships and keep in touch with their best lead sources: people.

- A real estate team may also help agents with expenses such as advertising, board dues, licensing fees, continuing education, and office bills.

Established agents will also benefit from a team. If a team is set up well, it will help an established agent sell more houses by providing support staff, leads, accountability, and help when an agent is sick or goes on vacation. Our goal is to let our agents sell houses while our staff takes care of the advertising, paperwork, and lead generation. I know I sell many more houses with a team and its help than I ever could on my own.

How can agents find a team?

The best way to find a real estate team is to find the agents who are selling the most houses in your area. The most successful agents usually have a team, and if they don't, they need one! Contact those agents who sell the most houses and see if they'll hire new agents or are looking for assistants to help. You can also check with different offices to see if there are real estate teams in their office that are looking for new agents. My real estate team in Northern Colorado (Greeley) is always looking for new agents. New agents who join our team must be highly motivated, available full-time, have a great work ethic, and be willing to talk on the phone a lot. A real estate team will help agents succeed, but agents must still work very hard. If you are interested in joining my team, send me an email: *mark@investfourmore.com.*

Joining a real estate team can be a huge boost to any real estate agent's career. Not every real estate team is the same, and not every team will provide the training and support agents are looking for. If you interview to join a real estate team, do more than answer their questions. Ask them what training they provide, what leads they provide, and how they will help you succeed. We do our best to help our agents succeed, but not all teams work the same way.

CHAPTER 21

How Does a Real Estate Agent Build a Database and Their Circle of Influence?

Agents make money from their circle of influence. Leads from Zillow and the internet can provide some sales, but nurturing your circle of influence and meeting people in person will bring you the most sales. Some of you (like me) may not be the most outgoing people and won't have a large circle of influence. You can create systems to make your real estate business run smoothly, and you can also create systems to meet more people and nurture existing relationships.

Most people like to do things that are comfortable to them. They like to hang out with people they know and do business with people they have already done business with. When someone must do business with a person they have never met, there will always be a certain level caution and discomfort until they trust the new person. For some people, it may take a day to trust someone new; for others, it may take years. When real estate agents get new leads from their website, an open house, or advertising, those leads are most likely strangers. The leads will not trust nor have any loyalty toward the agent until they get to know them.

If someone is looking to buy or sell a house and they know their agent on a personal level, they have already established trust and loyalty toward their agent. There is a much better chance personal relationship will end in a sale over a brand-new lead. The best way for agents to make a lot of money is to increase the number of people they know and nurture great relationships. Not only will people want to use an agent they know and care about, but they will also tell their friends and family to use that agent.

Tell everyone you know that you are a real estate agent

You have heard this over and over again, and that is because it is important! Do not be scared that your friends, family, or acquaintances will think you are trying to "sell" to them by telling them you are an agent. Most people are going to need an agent at some point in their lives, and you are providing them a service. Is it better for the people you know to use you as an agent, someone who will act in their best interests and do an awesome job? Or is it better to let your friends and family use an agent who may or may not have any idea what they are doing? By telling people you are an agent, you are helping people by selling houses for or to them.

If you have not talked to someone for a while and you are afraid it will sound like you only called to tell them you are an agent, tell them something else first. Call to talk and catch up on your lives. I guarantee at some point the other person is going to ask what you are doing now and how your life is going. This is the perfect chance to say you are going through a huge change in your life and just became an agent. There's no need to sell anyone; just talk about what is going on in your life, and you will have successfully told them you are in the business.

How do you create a system to meet people and nurture relationships?

My team works with a training program we created. It's all about building relationships. The more relationships you have, the more sales you will have and the more money you will make. Once you sell enough houses, you can hire a team, and they can start using systems to sell houses. Then you can drop your leads off to others and lessen your workload while making more money. It is a simple concept, and it works great.

A relationship-creating system must be written down, and you must hold yourself accountable to it. The best way to do this is to set goals every week for different tasks. How many people are you going to call each week? How many people are you going to see in person? How many people are you going to have lunch, coffee, or breakfast with? How many events or outings are you going to plan and invite people to?

Once you've set goals for how you'll meet people and nurture relationships, you must keep track of how you do. I don't mean keeping track, in your head, of how many people you think you called last week. Every day, you must write down how many people you called, how many people you saw, and how many people you met with. If you don't meet your goals, you need to think of a way to punish yourself.

What are good punishments for missing your goals?

Setting up punishments is a great way to force yourself to keep track of what you do. Building a habit takes about three weeks. After a couple days, most people quit or forget about something they start because it is not a habit yet. If you can keep doing the new task every day for three weeks, it will become a habit. Once you form a habit, completing the task and keeping it going becomes much easier.

One way to form a habit is to punish yourself for not doing what you are supposed to do. It must be a good punishment. If you decide to punish yourself by putting $10 in a jar that you can't touch for 6 months, that is not much of a punishment. You need to do something that hurts. Monetary punishments can work well, but often, we would rather lose a little money than make a few extra phone calls. You will do anything to avoid a good punishment. I can't tell you how to punish yourself. That's a very personal thing. However, one idea is to make a bet with a co-worker or friend. The other person decides what the punishment is, and they need to make sure it hurts.

How many people do you need to contact each week?

The more people you talk to, the more leads you will get and the more money you will make. The number of people you need to talk to is up to you, but it needs to be a lot! In a beginning program, each week you should call 60 people, go out to eat or have coffee with at least 5 people, meet face to face with at least 15 people, and hold 1 or 2 events. When you start bringing in business and can hire people to take care of leads, you need to increase the number of people you meet and talk to.

What are events and why are they important?

An event can be a happy hour at a bar or restaurant, a dinner party at your house, or a celebration at your office. The great thing about events is you meet a lot of people face to face, and it takes care of many of your weekly requirements for contacting people. An event must be hosted and paid for by you; you can't attend someone else's event. People remember who hosted a party...not all the guests.

Events are a great way to build real relationships. Talking on the phone for five minutes is great, but it is not the same as spending an hour with someone in person. Events are a great way to build meaningful relationships and gain lifelong clients.

Who do you call every week?

There are many people you can call each week to keep in touch.

- **Family:** close and extended, long-lost cousins, in laws, nieces, nephews, uncles, aunts etc.
- **Friends:** close friends, friends you lost touch with, and school mates. Facebook is great for this.
- **Co-workers:** people you work with now or have worked with in the past.
- **Business partners:** bankers, lawyers, accountants, dry cleaners, pet groomers, title companies, other real estate agents, property managers, and whoever you do business with.
- **Clients:** people you work with now or have worked with in the past

One of the hardest parts of the job is calling and meeting with people, but it's the most important part. The more you do it, the easier it will be and the more money you will make. Create a system to make yourself contact people, and it will be the best money you ever spent. Do this before you spend money on a website, advertising, or lead generation tools.

You must do more than just talk with people

Networking is a huge part of being a successful real estate agent, but there is much more to selling houses. Not only do you need to talk to as many people as you can, but you also need to keep track of who you talk to and follow up with them. One of the biggest mistakes agents make is not following up with potential clients. Not only do real estate agents have to follow up with clients who are in the process of buying or selling a house, but they also need to follow up with their circle of influence and all the people they talk to. The way to do this is to create a database.

A database will include everyone you know and will be sorted by how you know them, who they are, how important they are, and how often you will market to them. Many companies sell database software to real estate agents. Having and marketing a database is vitally important. Here are some ways to market to a database:

- Send email newsletters: This can include information on market trends and sales stats.
- Mail out sports schedules: These are usually magnets that can be hung on a fridge.
- Mail out interesting or useful info: These can include recipes, local events, and fun things to do.
- Invitations: These can be to happy hours or classes.
- Calling: Talk to your top people on a regular basis.
- Lunch or coffee: Call your top people and invite them to lunch or coffee on a regular basis.

One of any agent's main tasks should be growing their database and reminding people on that database that the agent exists and can help them with their real estate needs.

CHAPTER 22

Why Real Estate Agents Should Create Their Own Website

Many websites—Zillow, Trulia, Realtor.com, and more—try to sell real estate agents leads. Those websites promise the opportunity to produce buyer and seller leads without much work from the agent. Those websites do produce leads, but they are low-quality leads, and an agent can spend their money on much better things. We have tried many different lead sources. One of the best things we have ever done is create our own website that generates high-quality leads.

Why aren't the leads from Zillow and other websites very good?

We have obtained leads from Zillow for a couple of years. We have also tried Trulia and other lead-generating websites. The biggest problem with these sites is the way they generate leads. They sell agents on the quantity of leads and not the quality. Many of these sites generate leads by listing multiple agents for buyers to contact or by trying to get buyers to fill out forms for more information. These sites don't always make it clear that the buyer will be contacted by an agent when they fill out the forms.

To successfully convert these leads, agents must respond extremely fast. Even if they respond quickly, many buyers don't expect an agent to call them. Converting these leads takes quite a bit of explanation and constant communication because they have no idea who we are and have no loyalty to us. If you want to try Zillow and get 25% off of your Zillow premier membership, call 866-324-4005 and mention you were referred by Mark Ferguson. Full disclosure: I earn a $100 Amazon gift card if you use my name.

Why does an agent's own website generate more leads?

We have always had our own website, but we completely overhauled it a few months ago. In the past, our website was very similar to other agents' sites, with an IDX feed that allowed people to search for listings on the site. We did earn some leads, but when we changed the site, we completely eliminated the IDX feed. We changed the focus to our team and who we are. We have a blog containing many different articles related to the local real estate market. We advertise special programs and services offered by our team. We decided we did not need another website where people could search for house listings since there are about 10 million of them. I also thought that if people wanted to search for listings, they may not trust an agent's personal site since they may think it contains only the agent's listings.

When we made the switch, we thought it might take a few months or longer to see the results and start getting decent leads. It took about a week before the site generated leads. They have since bought or sold houses with us. They were looking for a real estate team, loved what they saw on our website, and wanted us to help them. The difference between a lead from our own website and a lead from lead-generating sites was like night and day. The great part is that eliminating IDX saves us a lot of money and makes the website much simpler. Since switching, our site has generated a steady stream of leads, and even though the site doesn't have much traffic, the lead quality is awesome.

If you want to check out our team website, visit: FergusonGreeley.com

How difficult is creating a website?

I am not very good at the technical side of websites. I know how to write articles, but I have no clue how to use HTML. I was able to start a blog because my friend helped me get started on WordPress. Since I started the blog, I have learned a lot about design and how WordPress works, but I am by no means an expert. If you have no idea how to build a website, don't give up.

Many companies can help you, and learning WordPress isn't too difficult. If you design your site yourself, building it and hosting it can be extremely cheap.

Creating a website is one thing, but actually getting traffic takes a little more work. I have had a ton of success with *Invest Four More*, mostly from writing about things I like to talk about. Many agents do not have time to write. I don't have time to write much for my own agent website. Writing blog articles is one way to get traffic, but you must be consistent. If you want to use a blog to gain traffic, you need to write at least a couple of articles per week, and they should be at least 750 words long. When you write an article, you need to share it on Facebook, Twitter, and any social media account you have. Don't expect to see a ton of traffic initially, as it can take months for Google to pick up any articles.

There are also ways to get traffic to your site without using Google or other search engines.

- **Facebook:** Not only can you post articles on Facebook, but you can also create ads, boost posts, and build a business page.
- **LinkedIn:** I loved LinkedIn when I first started my site. I posted articles in groups and posted updates as well.
- **Database**: Having a big database of past, current, and potential clients is vitally important. Send your database to your site, and give them valuable information to read.
- **Google Adwords**: This is how you advertise with Google. We use this to send traffic to our site.

Agents are bombarded with companies who want to sell us leads. I think agents should consider how they can create a valuable business. If you decide to retire or take some time off, would anyone care that you are paying Zillow $1,000 per month for leads? They could sign up with Zillow as well, but if you build an awesome website or an awesome database, you've built a sellable asset. Building a website takes a little more time and effort, but it will pay off in the end.

CHAPTER 23

To become a Successful Agent, You Must Take Care of Your Clients

We have discussed how to build relationships through networking, but once you get a client, the work is not over! The difference between the average real estate agent and the agent that makes a lot of money is how they take care of their clients.

Many agents are only concerned with selling individual houses to earn one commission. However, you can't be focused on earning only one commission—you must be focused on building a pipeline of customers. Successful agents do not focus on one sale at a time; they focus on making their customers as happy as possible, even if it means losing a commission. If an agent makes their clients happy, the clients will come back again and again. And, if you make your clients really happy, they will tell all their friends and family to use you.

Why is focusing only on sales a bad thing?

In the beginning, earning sales and generating income is tough. Therefore, prospective agents should have a good financial cushion. When you make very little money, one commission will seem like a lot. Many new agents will do anything to get a deal done, including pressuring their clients into buying or selling when it may not be the best choice.

It is very easy for new agents to get caught up in making a sale at all costs, but real estate is not about one sale, it is about building a customer base. Statistics show it is four times more expensive to find a new customer than it is to sell to an existing customer. If you focus on making the sale and not what is best for your client, you will lose that client. Finding new clients is always more difficult than keeping existing ones. Statistics also show 84% of buyers would use their past agent to buy a house again. If you only work for that one commission, you have a better chance of being in that 16 percent who don't receive repeat business.

Not only does taking care of your clients give you repeat business, but the clients you take care of will also tell their friends and family about you. The best free advertising you will ever get comes from satisfied customers. Most people will value a personal reference from a friend or family member much more than any advertising. Referrals from past clients are a great way to get new business, and those referrals will be more likely to buy from you than strangers who saw your real estate sign or an advertisement.

Don't just take care of the easy clients!

Clients who know exactly what they want and never complain about a thing are easy to please. Agents don't earn a great reputation by taking care of the easy clients. Making those people happy is easy, and just about any agent can take care of clients who don't require extra work.

Clients who always complain, always have a problem, and who are generally a pain need to be taken care of just as well as easy clients. Getting mad at difficult clients and ignoring their requests is easy because you may feel they deserve it or brought it on themselves. However, if you treat them right, difficult clients will become your biggest advocate. Easy clients might not even remember you because there was never a problem or a memorable event. Difficult clients will have many problems and many memorable events. They will remember how well or badly their agent treated them. If you leave them with good memories, they will be more likely to tell others about how awesome you are. Many people who are difficult to work with will not be used to people treating them well. If you go the extra mile for clients who don't deserve it, they will remember that.

A house is the biggest purchase most people will ever make

People rely on agents to help them through this massive purchase. It seems strange to me, but many people do not take buying a house that seriously. They think it is what most people do and it's not a big deal. It is a very big deal—and a very big decision. As agents, we must walk people through the process and assume they don't know what they are doing. You must use your knowledge to make the process painless for them. You must also make sure they understand the lending aspect, how much money they will need, and that house prices don't always go up. Don't assume your clients know what they are doing just because they don't ask questions.

How can real estate agents to go above and beyond for their clients?

- **Take a pay cut to get more listings**: Agents don't get paid a standard commission: all commissions are negotiable, but many agents charge specific amounts. In many cases, I will charge a smaller commission to repeat clients or to those who sell multiple houses. Taking care of those clients by charging a little less will earn me more money in the long run because they see value in using me, and I will sell more houses.

- **Take a pay cut to close a deal:** Sometimes a deal is nearly closed, but the buyer or seller can't agree on a minor issue. Lowering your commission to get the deal done makes sense in this case. Even if you earn a slightly smaller commission, it's better than nothing. Inspections and appraisals can cause a deal to fall apart, but a small commission reduction might keep these deals together. By lowering your commission so the deal will close, you make both the buyer and seller very happy.

- **Don't misrepresent values to get a listing or a sale:** Some sellers will pick a listing agent who recommends the highest sales price. To get a listing, some agents will suggest higher sales prices than the market will support. When the house doesn't sell for that amount, no one is happy. The seller may even fire the high-price agent and go with another agent. Being the agent that priced the house accurately is much better than being the one who lost the listing. Plus, you'll earn the seller's business again.

- **Don't misrepresent values to an investor:** Some agents may misrepresent the value of a fix and flip to get an investor to buy. They will say the after-repaired value will be more than it actually is in order to get the deal done. If the investor buys the house, makes repairs, and can't sell it, it's bad for everyone. If the agent misrepresented the possible sale price, you can be assured that investor will never use that agent again. The investor will also tell all his friends and investor buddies what happened. This could permanently taint the agent's reputation.

Conclusion

A lot of my suggestions involve lowering your commission, but I don't advocate lowering your commission on every deal where an issue arises. In some cases, a deal either cannot be saved or it makes more sense for your client to move on. In cases where reducing your commission to satisfy a client makes sense, you'll most likely make more money in the long run. Trading long-term referrals and clients for one check is never a good idea. Building a great real estate business takes time, and you must think about the long-term repercussions of all your actions.

CHAPTER 24

Why a Good Reputation Will Earn You More Money

Being an agent and investor, I hear a lot of stories about unethical business practices. I even hear people comparing real estate professionals to used-car salespeople. Unethical real estate agents and real estate investors definitely exist, but there are also many ethical and awesome people in the industry. I— and my father before me—have always done business the right way and have a good reputation in the community. Not only will a good reputation let you sleep well at night, but it can also make you more money.

Why does the real estate industry have a bad reputation?

Both real estate agents and real estate investors can give themselves a bad reputation. Not everyone in the industry is unethical, but when you are dealing with an asset like houses, doing the wrong thing gets a lot of attention...and rightly so. Most people remember when someone acts unethically, especially when it comes to such a big investment. Following are a few things real estate investors and real estate agents have done and do that are unethical.

Agents

Some agents focus on selling one house and earning one commission. In order to get that commission, they may not be totally honest with their clients. They may leave out important details or are not willing to advise their clients to terminate a deal, even if they know it is the best thing to do.

Some agents will not market a house to other agents as well as they should. They do this hoping they will find a buyer and earn both sides of the commission. This usually results in a lower selling price for the seller.

It's rare, but some agents will go as low as committing fraud against those who don't know any better. In my area, a group of agents met with builders, lenders, and appraisers and created a way to sell new houses for twice as much as they were worth. They did this by selling the houses to immigrants. The loans were short-term ARMs that had very small initial payments, and the appraisers used fraudulent appraisals to value the properties. The agents convinced the buyers they were getting a good deal. Luckily, many of the people involved in this scam went to jail.

Investors

Some real estate investors will prey on the seniors or the uninformed by buying their house for much less than it's worth. A great way to get deals it to buy off-market properties, but there is a fine line between ripping someone off and helping them unload their house.

New wholesalers tend to get houses under contract without doing all their homework or having real buyers. This causes them to cancel their contract and give good wholesalers a bad name. Many agents are very wary of any buyers who are also wholesalers because so many wholesalers don't follow through on their contracts.

Some investors will go to any means necessary to get a deal or save a few bucks. This could mean submitting hundreds of low-ball offers, always asking for a post-inspection price reduction, or screwing over agents who showed them houses to save some money on commissions. These tactics might save money in the short-term, but in the long run, it usually hurts you much more than it helps.

I have seen investors commit extreme fraud. Some investors have forged deeds or other documents to get properties. I know a couple of investors who went to jail for forging documents. Some investors have forged leases to show their properties are making more money than they actually are, which in turn would allow them to refinance the property for much more than it is worth. In some cases, the investors will then let these houses go into foreclosure.

Some rental-property owners are known as slumlords because they don't take care of their properties. This does not mean they have low-end rentals, just that they don't make repairs when needed or don't repair things right when they break.

Are all agents and investors unethical?

After that last section, you may think things look bleak in the real estate world, but not everyone is unethical. In all my years in the business, I've rarely seen unethical behavior. The truth is there are unethical people in every line of work, but when dealing with big dollar items like cars and houses, unethical behavior makes the news or is remembered.

When I see unethical behavior, it's usually from newer agents or investors who may not know any better. Agents involved in the most fraudulent activities tend not to be traditional agents, but rather people who obtained their real estate license just for that activity. Agents and investors who have made a lot of money in this business tend to treat people right and do the right thing. There are always some exceptions, but overall the agents that last are very ethical, and that helps them build their business.

How can agents and investors act ethically and build a good reputation?

Almost everyone thinks they are ethical, but when it comes to money, some people are more willing to cross the line than others. Knowing if you're ethical or not is pretty simple since most people know the difference between right and wrong. Many people, however, justify what they know is wrong through a variety of means:

- If someone else tells you it is okay to do something unethical, that does not make it okay! I see real estate investors use unethical tactics all the time because a real estate guru or other source told them someone else had successfully used the same tactics. If you break the law, the judge will not care if someone you never met told you it was okay. If you think a practice is unethical, use your own judgment...not someone else's.

- You already know agents must work under a broker. That broker is there to provide oversight and help. Any agent who is concerned about ethical matters should talk to their broker. The broker can help determine the right thing to do.

- If there is any possibility that what you are doing is unethical, ask a professional for their opinion. In most situations, if you have to ask someone else, you probably already know the answer. Some situations may toe the ethical line. In my experience, staying away from that line is best. The best way to get a good reputation is to do what is best for your clients and not yourself.

What have I done to promote my reputation?

Every situation is unique, but here are a few situations where my team went above and beyond (this may sound like bragging, but I will show you how it helps my business soon).

- Agents constantly deal with situations where buyers and sellers cannot agree on price but are very close. I have reduced my commission more than a few times to make a deal work. I have also paid for repairs or inspection items.

- After a flip is sold, we offer no guarantees on the work that is done. However, on multiple occasions, we've gone back to fix items the homeowner discovered after they bought the house. In some cases, like one that involved a broken sewer line, we did not even know about or cause the problem, but we pride ourselves on selling houses in great condition, so we repaired it.

- When I make offers on houses, I always follow through on unless something crazy comes up with the house. I do not ask for repairs upon inspection unless there is something major that could not be known before the inspection.

126

Making a lot of money in real estate is all about building for the long term. As an agent, you want to build a client base that will buy and sell houses with you over and over. You also want them to give referrals. If you sacrifice your clients' needs for short-term paychecks, you won't earn their repeat business. While you might make one commission check by acting in your own best interests, you will likely lose many more checks in the future.

As an investor, by always coming through on buying houses, other agents know that, when I make an offer, I will close. This allows me to get more deals because when agents have a seller who must sell a house quickly, they know I will not mess around with inspection issues or cancel half the offers I get accepted. Agents even bring great deals to me, asking if I would be interested in buying them. Agents remember both investors who are good to work with and ones who are not.

As an agent and investor, a good reputation helps me in two ways. When I repair a house after it closes or help bring a deal together by reducing my commission, I usually gain a new client. They may not buy or sell another house for years, but they usually tell their friends and family what I did and how I helped them.

Doing the right thing feels good and lets me sleep very well at night, but it also helps my business. In the long run, we are all better off doing the right thing, even if it hurts in the short-term.

CHAPTER 24

Can Real Estate Agents Make Money Working with Investors?

Most agents initially work with traditional buyers and sellers who are dealing with their personal residences. However, a great way for agents to sell more houses is by working with investors, although working with the wrong investors can be a huge waste of time. An agent can do many things to work with investors more effectively and to determine if an investor is worth working with. If you can find the right investors, you will close multiple deals and earn a great advocate.

Unlike me, many investors are not agents, and they need an agent to help them buy and sell properties. The great thing about investors is the good ones buy and sell multiple houses, which creates multiple commissions for an agent.

If you can work with investors who buy and sell many houses each year, it can be a very lucrative relationship. The hard part is finding the investors who do multiple deals each year and convincing them you are the right agent for them. Many investors use multiple agents or have an agent they have used for years. There is one way to get in with investors: make them money!

Investors love to find deals because deals earn them money. Finding a great deal will increase their cash flow on rental properties or allow them to make more money on a fix and flip. Finding an investor deals that will generate income is the way to get in good with them. The trick is finding these deals quickly.

One reason I am so successful getting deals from the MLS is I'm able to quickly view a house and make an offer. In fact, I can make an offer in less than two hours after a house hits the MLS. Often, I get a house under contract before any other investors make an offer.

Many investors have trouble finding an agent who will act fast. If I'm being honest, I don't act fast when working with investors, even though I'm an agent. I have too much going on between my rentals, fix and flips, and real estate team. Even though I am not a good agent for investors, my team can act very quickly and work great with investors. The faster you can send deals, show houses and write contracts, the more likely an investor will use you. If an investor must wait two days for their agent to write a contract, they may have already missed out on a great deal.

If you are a new agent looking to work with investors, you have a huge advantage. New agents have the time to search the MLS multiple times per day and immediately send investors potential deals. Experienced agents may have too many other clients and obligations to work fast enough.

Another thing agents can do to attract investors is find deals. If you can find deals, there is a good chance investors will use you. However, you must keep bringing them deals if you want to keep working with that investor.

Most agents simply do not know what an investor deems to be a good deal. Agents think that any house that is priced a little lower than market value will attract investors. Investors need to realize huge spreads in order to flip houses, and they need great cash flow to make money from rentals. It helps if the agent understands what kind of deal the investor needs. I have a lot of information on my blog, *InvestFourMore.com,* about investing in real estate. The more an agent can learn about investing in real estate, the better chance they have of working with an investor. If you really want to learn a lot about investing, there are also a few real estate investment books on my Amazon Author page.

If you can show an investor that you can act quickly, know the type of properties they are looking for, and can find them deals, you will have no problem finding investors to work with.

How do agents find investors?

Most investors are drawn to great deals and care more about the deal than the agent. I list HUD homes and REOs; both are usually full of great deals and attract investors. Listing REOs or HUD homes isn't easy, but that doesn't mean you can't find investors looking for great deals. As an agent, go where the deals are, and you will find the investors.

- **REIA clubs:** (Real Estate Investor Association) These clubs and meetups are full of investors.
- **Auctions:** Investors love auctions because they think they can find a great deal.
- **Foreclosure/trustee sales:** Many investors frequent these sales.
- **Word of mouth**: Agents should constantly network. Keep doing it, and you will meet investors.
- **Advertise other agents' listings:** Agents can advertise HUD homes, and many agents will let you hold open houses on their listings.

How do you know if an investor is really going to buy houses?

Many people want to be real estate investors. You can make a lot of money if you know what you are doing...and actually do it. However, most potential investors never buy an investment. They can't find the right deal, get distracted, don't have the money, won't put the work in, or haven't bought anything for other reasons. Separating good investors from the pretenders can be difficult. Here are a few tips to help you sort out the real investors from the wannabes:

- Do they own investment property? Do they have rentals, or have they flipped houses? If they have already done it, there is a good chance they will do it again.
- Does the investor know what they are talking about? Do they know what type of house they want, what price they will pay and what they'll make? The more they know, the more likely they will buy a house.
- Does the investor have money? Are they prequalified? If they are paying cash, do they have a proof-of-funds letter from their bank?
- Do they make reasonable offers? Some investors like to make offers that are 50 percent of the list price or lower. They tend to make a lot of these offers and hope one day a seller will accept one. Submitting an offer takes agents quite a bit of time, and even if an investor gets one of their lowball offers accepted, was all the work worth it?

Is it worth earning the reputation of being an agent who submits lowball offers on every listing?

- Does the investor look at hundreds of houses but never make an offer, even if the property meets their criteria?

You should consider all these things. Some investors will never buy a house, and others may buy hundreds. To save money, the investor who buys hundreds of houses may become an agent themselves, so don't be disappointed when that happens.

If you can work hard and find deals, investors will probably be a great source of income. But remember, investors are all about the bottom line, and when you start sending deals more slowly, send them fewer deals, or become too busy to help them, they will find a new agent in a heartbeat. Make sure your business is set up so you don't rely on just one investor because things can change quickly.

CHAPTER 25

What Does an REO Agent Do?

When I started my real estate career, I was not a good salesman. I was a natural introvert, and I did not like talking to people on the phone or in person. Since talking to strangers and selling them houses was a big part of my job, I did not sell many houses. I occasionally sold a house to my friends and family, but most of my income came from fix and flips that I completed with my father. Now that was an up-and-down income stream! I was not really happy being a traditional agent, but I did not have specific training to help me succeed, or maybe, I just didn't want to listen. Then I discovered the world of REO. Listing REO properties is completely different than listing traditional ones.

Even though I love REO yet am not great about talking to strangers, I still must use the techniques I discussed earlier to build relationships. In fact, I got into REO by cold-calling banks and asking them how to list their houses. It was not easy for me, but it was well worth it. I build all the relationships I can so I can deal with people I know rather than with strangers.

What is an REO property?

REO stands for Real Estate Owned and is the term banks use to describe houses they have repossessed through foreclosure. A house goes through foreclosure when a homeowner either stops making or falls behind on loan payments. In some states, foreclosure can take a few months, and in other states, it can take years. Once a house goes through the foreclosure process, the bank owns it and can sell it. An REO agent is a listing agent who sells REO properties for banks and asset managers. The asset manager is the main contact between the listing agent and the seller.

What does my REO business look like?

When I receive an REO listing, I get an email that says "new REO assignment," or something to that effect. All the instructions for handling the property are in emails, an attachment, and online. I rarely talk via phone to the bank or asset management company who sent me the listing. Almost all of our communication is through email, and I get a steady stream of listings without having to cold call, hold open houses, send out mailers, or make sure I am available to answer every single incoming call (agents on my team do send out flyers, and we hold happy hours every month for our clients).

I also complete many BPOs (Broker Price Opinions) for banks and asset management companies, which also require very little contact. I receive the order, complete it, and earn $40 to $100 for each report. I'm not the only one who prefers to complete work online with minimal distractions: most banks also prefer email and quick communication. Once I entered the REO and BPO world, I knew I had found the perfect fit!

Over the last three years, I have sold over 400 REOs and HUD homes. I have been a Realtor since 2001, and I have specialized in REOs since 2008. I did well as a traditional Realtor, but I have excelled since I starting to list REO properties. Like most rewarding endeavors, listing REO properties isn't easy. Becoming an REO broker takes time, persistence, money, and hard work. If you are able to break through and become a successful REO broker, you'll earn great money and freedom, which is hard to beat.

When I started to get involved with REO, I had no mentor or guidance. My father had been an agent since 1978, but he never did REO. I started cold-calling banks to find out where to start (that was difficult for me, but I did it!). Luckily, a few banks pointed me in the right direction, and I was able to get a couple of listings relatively quickly. Things started to snowball, and pretty soon, I was a full-blown REO agent! I made a lot of mistakes along the way and missed out on some huge clients due to my ignorance. If only I had known then what I know now! If you are interested in becoming an REO or BPO agent, I highly suggest my REO starter kit. It will help you avoid the mistakes I made and get business quickly. You won't have to guess or work through trial and error.

My REO starter kit will give you all the tips and tricks I have used to list REO properties and HUD homes. It is not as easy as listing homes on the MLS and collecting a commission check.

My REO kit includes a detailed guide, videos, sample resume, HUD guide, and access to email coaching where I will personally answer your REO questions.

How much money can you make when you list REO properties?

In the chapter titled "How Much Money Do Real Estate Agents Make?" I provide full details on how much a REO agent makes. As a brief reminder, I sold around 150 REO and HUD properties in 2013, 127 in 2012, and 184 in 2011. The average commission I receive from banks on an REO property is around 2.5%, and HUD pays listing agents a 3% commission. My average sales price was about $120,000 last year, which equates to over $400,000 in REO gross income.

Investing and REO

I consider myself an REO broker first and an investor second. I love investing in real estate, and REO properties are one of the reasons I have made enough money to buy 16 rental properties in the last 5 years.

Many people think I have a huge advantage because I list REO properties. The truth is it actually hurts me much more than it helps me. Basically, there are many properties I cannot buy because I list both REO and HUD properties. As a HUD listing broker, I cannot buy any HUD homes. There are other banks that prohibit me from buying their listings, and I cannot buy any of my own listings.

Is this a good time to list REO properties?

Many people believe the REO listing business is dead because there are fewer and fewer foreclosures every year. While REO listings are diminishing, the business always goes in cycles. It's actually a great time to list REO properties because the fewer REOs there are, the fewer REO agents there are. When inventory and competition are low, REO properties offer the best opportunities. Asset managers don't want fly-by-night agents who disappear when inventory falls. They want the great REO agents who will help them no matter what the market does.

There will always be REO properties. Some years, there will be more than others. Even if REO listings fall within the next year or two, we will see them rise again when the cycle turns. When the economy struggles or housing prices drop, REO listings will increase.

Every market is also different. In Colorado, we do not have many REOs at all. In Florida and New Jersey, there are thousands and thousands. Some of the most successful REO agents in the country have offices in multiple parts of the country to take advantage of rising and falling REO inventories.

What does an REO broker do?

Many traditional agents tend to think listing REO properties is a pretty easy job. You simply get listings, put them on the MLS, submit offers, and collect a check. In actuality, it's a lot of work! Working with banks is much different from working with a traditional seller. REO brokers work with out-of-state sellers who never see the property. We must be the seller's eyes, ears, and nose. Here is some of what you must do when you list REO properties.

1. Inspect the property

An REO agent must constantly inspect properties. The properties are most likely vacant and have a better chance of being vandalized than an occupied property. Most banks and HUD require weekly inspections. They also require an initial inspection within 24 hours of the property being assigned.

2. Maintenance and repairs

When you list REO properties, banks will expect you to hire contractors to maintain them and complete any repairs. This includes rekeys, winterizations, yard maintenance, and in some cases, full rehabs. When doing certain repairs, we must obtain at least two or even three bids before the work can be done. If the work will cost more than the bid, we must receive prior approval before any additions can be made. We are not allowed to use any friends or family for the work.

3. Fronting money

Many banks also expect the REO agent to pay the contractors for any completed work. The REO broker then must submit invoices to the bank with proof the work was completed, including before-and-after pictures and wait for the bank to reimburse them. An REO agent can have $10,000 or more in outstanding invoices per property! Many REO brokers have problems with banks not paying back reimbursements in a timely manner—or at all. We must keep very good track of invoices and make sure we are paid back. Some banks even charge us processing fees for paying their bills for them.

4. Scope of repairs

Banks require an REO agent to be knowledgeable about repairs and repair costs. Whenever I receive a new assignment, I must walk through a house, note any items that need repairing, take pictures, and calculate the repair costs.

5. Pictures, pictures, pictures!

I must take pictures of everything, including every room, each exterior side, the yard, the address, street scenes, and sometimes neighboring properties. Most pictures must be date stamped, but listing pictures should not be. I literally have thousands and thousands of pictures on my computer.

6. BPOs

A BPO (Broker Price Opinion) is like an appraisal but performed by an agent. A BPO consists of sold comps, active comps, subject details, and commentary explaining the subject, comps, and values. Banks require comparable properties to be within a certain age, square footage, and distance from the subject. They also prefer similar bedroom count, style, and condition. Many forms will also require adjustments to be made for any differences between the subject and the comps. Whenever I list REO properties, I must also complete a BPO on the property.

7. Cash for keys and evictions

One of the most difficult jobs when listing REO properties is completing cash for keys and evictions. Cash for keys occurs when a bank forecloses on a property, but the previous owners or tenants still live in the property. The bank will usually offer the occupants a certain amount of money to move out by a specific date. Often, they will offer twice the property's market rent to move out within 30 days.

When the occupants move out, they must take all personal belongings and clean the house. If they do not clean or remove everything, the REO agent shouldn't pay the occupants. If the REO agent does pay and the house is not clean, the bank may charge the agent for the cleaning! If the cash for keys agreement can't be worked out, the bank will evict. The REO broker must coordinate the eviction with both the sheriff and the clean-out crew. The REO broker must be there for the eviction and oversee everything.

8. Listing a property

Finally, we get to list the REO property! When we get a listing from the bank, they give us 24 hours to list it in the MLS and send the MLS sheet back to the bank. Most banks want to convey certain wording, through the MLS, to the public or other agents. We are supposed to write a detailed marketing description and treat the listing as if the bank were a traditional seller who wants the house portrayed positively. We must upload multiple pictures, room measurements, and other pertinent information. Some banks will require the sign and marketing materials (flyers) to be displayed at the property, and once the listing agreement is sent, the bank will require pictures within 24 hours.

9. Submitting Offers

If a house is priced correctly, we usually get offers right away, and sometimes we get multiple offers. Sellers loves multiple offers because they can try to get people into a bidding war. However, the REO broker sees a lot of work ahead whenever there are multiple offers. With each offer, the agent must submit either the entire offer or the terms of the offer to the bank depending on the system the bank uses. Once an offer is submitted, we wait for the bank to respond, and we convey that to the buyer's agent. When we receive multiple offers, we must submit those to the bank, and send multiple offer forms to all agents involved. We then wait for new offers to come in and resubmit all the offers again. Depending on the system the bank uses, submitting an offer can take anywhere from 5 to 20 minutes. Submitting 25 offers is really fun!

10. Inspections and appraisal

With many banks, the REO broker is responsible for turning on the water and all other utilities for inspections and appraisals. We must meet the city or utility company, turn everything on, and, in the winter, have the property re-winterized.

11. Closings, loans, etc.

During the under-contract phase, the listing agent must update the bank on the buyer's loan process, inspection, appraisal, and any other issues that come up. If there are appraisal requirements, inspection requirements, or lender problems, we must communicate with the bank and buyer's agent and come up with solutions. Many banks won't make repairs, even for appraisal requirements. In those cases, the house goes back on the market, and the entire process starts over again.

12. Selling

We made it to closing! Some banks require the REO broker to be at closing and some do not. I prefer not to be there due to the time it takes, especially when my closings range from across the street to 50 miles away. I can also do more to solve a problem at my desk in the office than I can at a closing. After closing, we must retrieve our lockbox and sign, take the utilities out of our name, and get all invoices into the bank ASAP.

13. Timelines

The last and most-important thing to know when you list REO properties is the bank's timelines. Each bank has different requirements for when tasks are due, but completing those tasks on time is very important. I usually get 24 hours for initial inspection, 48 hours for BPOS, 24 hours for MLS sheets, and 72 hours for HOA info. But, there are many, many more tasks. If you do not complete tasks on time, the bank will find someone who does. Many agents want to get into REO, and banks do not have to look far to find a replacement.

14. Teaching

Yes, I am also a teacher. As a HUD listing broker, I am required to teach at least one class per month. I teach agents, buyers, and the public. My agent classes are actually approved for continuing education credits for real estate agents. One of my biggest jobs is teaching agents how to submit offers through the HUD system.

15. Communication

Communication is huge for an REO broker. We are basically on call 7 days a week. If they need something, asset managers will call or email us at all times of the day and on the weekends. They expect us to get back to them within the same day, if not within a couple of hours. I work many weekends because I receive new assignments on Friday and Saturday night. I have 24 hours to complete tasks, not 24 business hours. Many buyers and agents also contact me constantly. I must be good on the phone, even though I try to get people to email me as much as possible.

Becoming an REO broker

Becoming an REO broker is not easy by any means. When I started out, I began calling banks, asking them how to list REO properties for them. Some of the banks were actually nice enough to tell me what I needed to do, and some would not talk to me at all. Building my business and getting to where I am today took years. If you can do it, it is highly rewarding, but it won't happen overnight. For me, it is a perfect job because I can use email as my primary communication tool and have my staff do most of my tasks.

Building your business to the point where you can work REO can also take years. The great thing about real estate is there are multiple ways to make money, from selling traditional houses to referring buyers to agents in other states.

CHAPTER 26

How to Complete a Broker Price Opinion (BPO)

As an REO agent, one of my main tasks is to complete Broker Price Opinions. When I get a new REO assignment, I must complete at least one, or in some case multiple, BPOs on that property. I also complete paid BPOs on many properties that are not my listings. Completing a great BPO will help you get more REO listings and get you more business with paid BPO companies. Finishing a good BPO in a timely manner takes time. Not only can BPOs help you get REO business, but they can also help you learn values in your area and can be a great tool for obtaining traditional listings. Most listing brokers have no idea how to complete a BPO and will provide a CMA (Competitive Market Analysis) for sellers. A CMA does not have nearly as much information as a BPO, which is more like an appraisal.

What is a BPO?

A BPO is a report that is like an appraisal and is compiled by a licensed real estate agent. A BPO is not an appraisal, and only licensed appraisers can complete appraisals. In fact, some states have made it illegal for real estate agents to complete BPOs, so always check with your state laws before completing BPOs.

Here is what will be needed for each BPO:

- Exterior or interior pictures depending on the type of BPO. Interior BPOs require the agent to inspect the interior of the property, and they usually pay more than exterior BPOs. Exterior BPOs require pictures of the property be taken from the street.
- Three comparable sold properties and three listed comparable properties. You will have to find comps

that are similar to the subject property and enter data for those comps in the BPO form.

- Subject property data also must be entered. This includes square footage, room count, type of property, tax ID numbers, location (rural, suburban, urban), condition, and amenities (AC, deck, pool, etc.).
- You will have to enter extensive comments that describes the property you are valuing, the comparable properties, the neighborhood, the market, and how you came up with your value.
- Many BPO forms require the agent to make adjustments to the comparable properties. If the subject has different features than the comparable properties, you would adjust the sold or listed price of the comparable property like an appraiser would. If the subject has AC and the comp does not, you would have to add value to the comp property.
- Some companies also require the agent to upload MLS sheets or public-records information to confirm the information entered was correct.

How long does completing a BPO take?

When I complete BPOs, I can finish the report in about 20 to 30 minutes, and that includes pulling comps and entering data. I have done thousands of BPOs, and I am much faster than most beginners. At this point in my real estate career, I have my assistants complete the BPOs, and they have become as fast as me. When they first started, it would take them over an hour in many cases to complete the report.

As my team performed more and more BPOs, they got faster and faster. They learned to pull comp data more quickly and enter data and write comments more quickly. If you are getting paid $50 for a BPO and it takes you two hours, it may not be worth your time because you must drive to the property and inspect it as well. If you can complete the report in 30 minutes or less, and you are getting a lot of orders, you can make a good living.

Completing inspections on BPOs can take up a lot of time. If you are getting one or two orders a week and the properties are 20 miles away, you'll spend a lot of time and use a lot of gas. You must make sure you consider the drive time. I would not accept orders over 30 minutes away unless the BPO company agreed to pay more or I had multiple orders in the same area. When I started getting a lot of orders, I would wait a day or two to complete pictures so that I could drive by as many properties in one trip as possible to save time.

If you get a new REO assignment and must complete a BPO, visit the property as soon as possible, and complete the BPO as soon as possible.

How much do you get paid for completing BPOs?

Most clients will pay about $50 for an exterior BPO and about $75 for an interior one. Some companies pay less and some more. BPO prices have gone down over the last few years as BPO companies try to save time and money. Some companies pay as little as $30 for an exterior order. I will not accept any orders that are less than $40, and those orders must be very close to me. For interior orders, I expect at least $70 for it to be worth our time.

In some cases, the properties will be in very rural areas, and BPO companies will be willing to negotiate. I have earned $150 for orders located an hour away. That's not worth it for me, but in some cases, BPO companies will let you hire a runner to take pictures for you. If you are doing interior inspections, you must be a licensed agent.

How much can you earn by completing BPOs?

Income of $50 a couple of times per week does not add up very fast, but you can complete a lot of orders when you get used to the work. In one year, I have completed over 1,000 BPO orders and grossed close to $50,000. I was not even doing BPOs full-time; I also was listing and selling REOs. The BPO income was a bonus. You probably won't be able to complete 1,000 BPOs in your first year. Like most other parts of real estate, building business, finding clients, and earning a good reputation takes time. On the other hand, getting BPO business is much easier than getting REO listings. Completing good BPOs can lead to getting REO listings.

How can completing BPOs lead to REO listings?

On every REO listing an agent receives, they must complete a BPO. They do not get paid for doing the BPOs because it is considered part of the listing job. Many companies and banks that have REO listings also use agents to complete BPOs that are not associated with REO listings. If you do an awesome job on the company's BPOs, you will have the best shot of selling REOs for them if they need an agent in your area.

When you complete BPOs for companies that only do BPOs and do not have REO listings, you still have a chance of getting REO listings. Your name is on each BPO you complete, and that BPO eventually makes its way to the property owner. There is a pretty small chance the property owner, whether it is a bank, hedge fund, or the government, will use the agent just because they completed a BPO, but it has happened. One of the best ways to get REO clients is by getting your name out there as much as possible.

One of the biggest challenges to earning REO business is banks and asset-management companies want to use experienced REO agents. If you have never listed an REO property, getting any REO listings is difficult. If you can't get any REO listings, getting experience is tough. If you complete BPOs, you show you are in the REO industry, and you have a much better chance of obtaining REOs than if you have no experience at all.

How to find REO and BPO companies

You can search for BPO and REO companies online, but sorting through all the fake companies and knowing which companies actually have business is tough. Many companies claim they can get you REO and BPO business, but they won't have connections to the banks and will only take your money. Some decent companies do have connections and will help you get REO and BPO business. For BPOs, I suggest signing up with

NABPOP. They are a reputable company with a huge list of BPO companies. I also offer a list of REO and BPO companies in my REO kit.

CHAPTER 27

Is Property Management a Good Business for Agents?

Many prospective agents have asked me—and wondered to themselves—if working in property management is a good way to get started. When you work with a property manager, they will most likely pay you a salary or wages, and you will gain experience with managing properties. As a bonus, many property management companies will let agents sell properties on the side under the property management brokerage.

Even though you would get paid regularly and earn some experience selling houses, I don't think starting in property management is the way to make a lot of money in real estate. If you want to be a successful agent, you need to focus on selling houses from day one.

How much money do property managers make?

Property managers get paid by taking a percentage of the rents on the properties they manage. They may earn 8, 10, or 12 percent for managing properties (the amounts can vary). Some property managers will also charge leasing fees, which may be one month's or a half month's rent. Most property managers do not make a lot of money unless they manage a lot of properties.

If a property manager managed 100 properties and received 10 percent of the rents, they would make $10,000 per month assuming rents of $1,000 per month. That is a decent amount of money, but there is a lot of work involved in managing 100 properties, and all those properties won't be rented out every month, which reduces the amount the property manager makes. It would also take a very long time to build up a business that manages 100 proprieties in most markets. There would be many expenses that come along with a physical business, like marketing, rent, utilities, and more.

A property manager must rent out houses, collect rent, screen tenants, manage repairs, keep track of accounting, and complete many other tasks. Many property managers need help when they start managing 100 properties or more because it is a lot of work. If you want to work for a property manager to begin your real estate career, you may get a steady paycheck, but it won't be a big check. Most property managers do not make a lot of money and will not have a lot of money to pay their staff.

An agent who works for a property manager will be lucky to make anything more than $12 per hour. My sister ran a property management company for years, and she had a lot of turnover. In fact, one of the members on my team worked for her property management company before she joined my team. She hated working in property management! She hated dealing with tenants, repairs, and the phone calls that come in the middle of the night. I am not saying everyone will hate property management, but it is more of a job than a career. Dealing with tenants, contractors, and paperwork is not fun, especially when you must do it for other people's properties.

If you own your own rental properties and manage them, it is a lot more fun because you should be making a lot more money!

What kind of training will property managers provide?

It is very important for new agents to receive a lot of training, and if possible, have a mentor. However, you want a mentor that knows how to sell houses, not manage rental properties. Unless your dream is to manage rental properties, you will make much more money selling houses. If you want to be an agent and make money selling houses, learning from someone who doesn't specialize in selling houses doesn't make sense.

Even though property managers sell some houses, most of those houses involve the properties they manage. Property managers don't usually market for buyers or sellers but will list a house for a landlord. In fact, some property management companies will have a clause in their contract with landlords saying the landlord must sell their house through the property management company if they list it. While you may learn how a property management company sells houses, most new agents won't be able to use their techniques unless they are a property manager.

Will property managers have time to train new agents?

Property managers will have to train anyone that works for them, but they train them on managing rental properties. Most people do not have the time to train people correctly, so don't expect them to also train you to do a job you were not hired for. Do not expect training specific to selling houses because that is not the property manager's specialty, and they won't have the time for it.

If you are working for a property management company, selling houses on the side will be difficult. In fact, selling houses part-time is difficult with any type of job. Clients will want to see houses at different times of the day and week. They will not want to wait until the weekend or until you get off work.

What alternatives are there for new agents?

If you want some type of paycheck when you become an agent, you have more options than property management. The best option is to join a successful real estate team, and they may possibly pay you hourly to perform certain tasks. When you join a successful team, you know you are in an environment where the focus is on selling houses, not renting them. You also know you will be learning from agents who sell many houses per year, know how to market themselves, and know how to get clients.

If you want to become a successful real estate agent, you want to focus all your time and effort on building your business. Working part-time or for a company that does not focus on your desired niche will slow the process. Find a real estate team, not a property manager, and you will become much more successful more quickly.

CHAPTER 28

To Be a Great Agent, You Must Be an Entrepreneur

To be a successful agent, you must act like an entrepreneur because you are essentially running a business. The freedom real estate offers is fantastic, but that freedom also means must to motivate yourself and make yourself successful. This may scare people who are used to a boss telling them what to do, but having control of your own destiny is a both great feeling and a great opportunity...if you embrace it.

One of the great things about being an agent is you run your own business but without all the responsibility of owning a business. In every state, you must work under a broker when you start your career. That broker is responsible for providing staff, choosing a location, buying supplies, and many other things that a business owner must do. Agents under that broker are responsible for finding business and closing deals, but they don't have to worry about running the office.

Why can't you treat being an agent as a regular job?

Most jobs give you tasks you must complete and pay employees by the hour or through a salary. Do what you are asked to do, and you will probably keep your job. Go above and beyond, and you might get a promotion. However, no one is there to tell an agent what to do all the time (depending on your office and broker). You may get some oversight and direction, but making sure you do the work is up to you. If you don't push yourself to do the work, and to do the right type of work, becoming a successful agent will be difficult.

Doing the right type of work is very important

Doing the right work, and not just any work, is one of the biggest challenges agents face. Agents can do many things, including education, direct mailing, phone calls, reaching out to your friends and family, and much more. Many agents get caught up doing the easy things. They plan, take classes, and constantly prepare, but they don't do the part of the job that makes money: talking to as many people as possible. Telling everyone you are an agent and going after clients that don't know you is one of your most important tasks. You must ensure you are doing everything you can to get business, which involves going far beyond the prep work.

I see many agents focusing on online leads or taking classes instead of picking up the phone or meeting people. Even if you are brand new and have no clue what you are doing, you need to talk to people. The best way to learn something is to do it.

Your own plan will make you more successful

To make yourself a successful agent, you must have goals and a plan. I have many goals and many plans that I am constantly reviewing and changing. Those goals and plans remind me what I am going after, what my end game is, and why I am doing the difficult work.

One of the great things about being an entrepreneur is creating your own plan. When you create your own plan, you have a better chance of being successful because it is yours and you made it. Following someone else's plan, which many of us do when we work for someone else, isn't motivational. Plus, we may not even know the entire plan—just our little part in it. By creating our own plan, we take control, can see the entire plan, and we know if we screw up, it is only our fault!

Building a team and a business

Earlier, I discussed why becoming an entrepreneurial agent is great. You don't have to manage everything like the broker or office owner does. The typical business owner will have much more on their plate than an agent. That does not mean you can't take more control and make more money as you become more experienced.

When you become more successful, you should think about creating a team. You don't have to start your own office to have your own team, as most brokers allow teams. A team allows you to delegate tasks you do not like and to make money off other agents. The sooner you build a team, the sooner you will make more money and have more time.

Once you have mastered running a team, you can start your own office and take complete control. The beauty of being a real estate agent is you can slowly acclimate to the entrepreneurial world without jumping all the way in.

You are treated as an entrepreneur by the IRS and others

Another reason to act as an entrepreneur is the IRS treats you as one. You are self-employed; you must keep track of expenses; and taxes aren't deducted from your paycheck. You must save money for taxes, paying them quarterly is smart so you are not hit with a huge tax bill at the end of the year.

You also will not get benefits, health insurance, or a 401k in most cases. You must plan your own retirement and save money without help. This may scare a lot of people, but if you really want to get ahead in life, you must be willing to do what others won't.

Being a real estate agent is a fantastic business opportunity for those who are willing to work hard and treat it as a business. If you want a steady income and clear tasks presented to you every day, real estate may not be for you. If you want to make a lot of money and have a lot of free time, real estate provides a great opportunity.

CHAPTER 29

Why Everyone Should Use a Real Estate Agent to Sell Their House

This may seem like a strange chapter to put in a book that is geared towards getting business as an agent. Hopefully, as a prospective agent, you already know the value you bring to a seller or a buyer. However, you are sure to run into people who think they can sell their house themselves and save money. The truth is real estate agents are expensive because they are worth it. You can use this chapter to help convince a seller why agents are so valuable.

Using an agent can be expensive, and many sellers think selling a house themselves is a great way to save money. A seller may save a commission, but trying to sell a house without an agent may actually cost the seller more money than the commission they saved. People will claim they saved thousands by selling their house themselves, and they'll even claim they sold it in one day! There is a reason they sold it in one day: they left a lot of money on the table! A great agent could have more than made up for the commission they charged by pricing a house correctly and working for the seller's best interest. While an agent's commissions may seem high, knowing they're negotiable is important. Agents justify charging so much because they provide a great value and usually get the buyers much more money than they could on their own.

Agents are marketing experts, and they know the sales process and know how to value a house. This is exactly why real estate agents get paid so much. They are not paid just for the time they spend selling your house. They are paid for all the licensing courses and continuing education they must take. They are paid for their experience marketing homes and getting the seller the most money possible.

When you sell a house yourself, you may not save as much as you think

You may think you can save 5, 6, or even 7 percent of the sales price by not paying a commission (all commissions are negotiable). However, most buyers work with agents when looking for a house. If you don't pay the agent representing the buyer a commission, you eliminate most of the buyers in your market. Eliminating most buyers will hurt your selling price and cost you money. If you do agree to pay a cooperating broker, you only save half of a commission. Additionally, the buyer is represented by a real estate agent and you are not. Who will have the upper hand during negotiations and the selling process? The buyer's agent will have the best interest of the buyer in mind...not yours.

Why is valuing a house correctly so important?

If you either price a house too low or overprice it, you could lose thousands. The best opportunity to receive a great offer is when a house first goes on the market, especially in today's seller's market. Buyers are waiting for the perfect house to come up for sale, and pricing the house correctly from the onset is vital. Here is a great statistic for people who try to sell a house themselves versus using a real estate agent:

FSBOs (for sale by owner) accounted for 9% of house sales in 2012. The typical FSBO house sold for $174,900, compared to $215,000 for agent-assisted home sales.

From http://www.realtor.org/field-guides/field-guide-to-quick-real-estate-statistics

Why will overpricing a house cost a seller money?

If an overpriced house comes on the market, a buyer may not even look at it. An overpriced house will sit there for weeks, or maybe even months, until the price is lowered. When buyers learn a house has been on the market for an extended period, they start to wonder what is wrong with it. Even if the price is lowered to the right value after a few weeks, the house still may not sell for what it would have sold for if it had been valued correctly to begin with. Houses become stigmatized the longer they are on the market. For an investor or a homeowner who no longer occupies the property, a stigmatized listing is very bad. Every month a house sits vacant costs the seller money, and if there is a loan on the house, it can cost the seller thousands of dollars per month. If the seller had priced it correctly to begin with, they would have sold the house quickly and saved thousands of dollars.

How will pricing a house too low cost a seller money?

Pricing a house too low can cost the seller just as much money as overpricing it. When you underprice a house, you will most likely sell it very quickly, but there is a great chance you will sell it for less than it is worth. Sure, underpricing a house can stir up a lot of activity and produce many offers. In a multiple-offer situation, getting a contract over asking price is possible. The problem with a low asking price is it attracts buyers, like myself, who want a great deal. Often, a multiple-offer situation will actually scare away some buyers. They do not want to get into a bidding war and will not bid on a house that has multiple offers.

If you price a house too low and get an offer over asking price, chances are you could have gotten an even higher offer had you priced it correctly. Most buyers will base their offer off the list price and not what the house is actually worth. Buyers always tell me, "I offered $10,000 over asking price and still did not get the house!" However, they are basing their offer on the list price, assuming the seller is asking fair-market value. They are not basing their offer on what the house may be worth. Another downside to offers that well exceed the asking price is they may give an appraiser a reason to come in low. If an appraisal comes in low, the seller could lose even more money! By pricing the house correctly to begin with, you will almost always sell it for the most money.

Why is valuing a house yourself difficult?

Valuing a property is the most important aspect of selling a house. Without a lot of experience and MLS access, it is very difficult. And, without MLS access, getting information about recently sold properties is very difficult. Recently sold properties are the most important piece of information needed to value a house. People have access to active listings through websites like Zillow, but only licensed agents have access to the MLS, which lists sold houses. Active listings can give an idea of house values, but you have no idea if they are overpriced or for what price they will actually sell. Every house has different features. And, location affects value as well. Agents are experts at determining value based off these characteristics. Understanding local markets can take years, and local markets can change extremely fast. Determining value correctly takes an agent a lot of time, and it isn't easy. It is much more difficult for someone who is not an agent.

How accurate is Zillow?

Zillow provides a house-value "Zestimate." Many people think this value is accurate, but it can be way off. Zillow was off by as much as 40% on one of my properties! You should never value a house based solely on a Zestimate.

An agent knows how to deal with a low appraisal

If you end up with a buyer who is getting a loan, they will most likely need an appraisal. The bank will lend based on that appraisal, and if the appraisal comes in low, there is a good chance the buyer will need the price of the house to be lowered. With rising house prices, we see appraisals come in low all the time, and there is a way to deal with appraisers. An agent knows how to proactively help the appraiser and knows how to challenge an appraisal if it comes in low.

An agent knows how to market a house

There is a definite art to marketing a house correctly. You can't just stick a house in the MLS and wait for offers to come in (unless you price it too low). Agents know how to take the best pictures, do virtual tours, create the best brochures, which websites to use, which magazines and newspapers to advertise in, and much more. Agents also know people and have their own list to market to. Often, an agent will know buyers who are waiting for a house just like yours.

Why can't a seller use a low-fee service to enter a house in the MLS?

Many companies now offer low-fee MLS services, where you pay a couple hundred dollars to have your house entered in the MLS. Using this type of service poses many problems:

- The service may never see your house and may enter incorrect information without pictures.
- The seller must still take calls and set up showings with many of these services.
- You will have to pay the buyer's agent if you enter the house in the MLS. Once you pay the MLS listing company and buyer's agent, are you really saving much money?
- You still aren't represented by an agent while the buyer is, so you won't receive help with contracts, negotiations, inspections, appraisals, etc.

Agents know how to handle state contracts

Speaking of contracts, have you seen your state contract recently? In Colorado, the contract is 17 pages long, which doesn't include the four required addendums and disclosures. Agents know exactly what to look for. They also know what the buyers and sellers customarily pay. In Colorado, the seller customarily pays for title insurance and many other costs to be split by the buyer and the seller. The buyer also pays many costs.

If you do not have an agent to help you know what a seller pays, you could easily pay many more costs than you should.

Agents know title companies, lenders, and other agents

Agents know the market, and they also know people in the business. They can help a seller find a title company with the lowest fees and best service. They can help the seller find the best contractor if repairs are needed before the listing or after an inspection. Here are a few more things an agent will help a seller with:

- Negotiating price
- Negotiating inspections
- Negotiating appraisals
- Negotiating title resolutions
- Negotiating multiple offers
- Negotiating seller concessions
- Negotiating earnest money
- Negotiating inclusions and exclusions
- Negotiating conditional sale contingencies
- Negotiating survey resolutions
- Negotiating due diligence resolutions
- Obtaining and reviewing buyer qualification letters
- Negotiating closing and possession dates

Conclusion

It is almost always better to sell your house through an agent rather than yourself. An agent will make you more money on the sale due to their knowledge and experience. I know many investors who have their real estate license, and they still use another agent to sell their house for them. Those investors know that another agent has the time and market expertise needed to sell the house. Before you try to sell on your own, consider if it is worth the time it will take to understand the process, and consider if you will actually save any money.

PART 4

CHAPTER 30

How to Run Your Business Better by Hiring Help and Delegating Tasks

You can be a successful agent and make a great living on your own, but everyone is limited by the time they have. Selling 100 houses each year will take a lot of time and a lot of paperwork. I don't like paperwork; I don't like talking to title companies; and I don't like showing houses. Clearly, there are a lot of things about real estate that I don't like! The great part about being an entrepreneur is I can hire people to do the tasks I do not like, and I concentrate on the fun stuff. Not only do I enjoy the work more because I choose to do the work I enjoy, but I also make more money by hiring help.

You run a real estate team just like you run a business. In order to run profitable businesses that grow into something big, you must learn to hire great people and delegate tasks. My business took off after I hired a great assistant and started to let other people do the busy work. In fact, the people you hire may be better at doing those delegated tasks than you are. That means your service and quality of work will improve by letting others work for you.

My experience with running a real estate team

When I first hired an assistant, I knew I needed help. I was drowning in tasks and working 10- to 12- hour days, including the weekends. It was apparent something had to change before I burned out or started making mistakes. After I hired my first assistant, my workload decreased significantly. I saw how many tasks I was simply ignoring because I was so busy. I had been stuck doing day-to-day tasks to keep my business going, and I forgot about going after new business or improving my systems. While one part of my business was doing awesome (REO), the other parts were doing worse (flips) because I had neglected them. I didn't want to neglect them, but I simply did not have enough time in the day to do everything.

The first thing hiring an assistant did was allow me to spend time improving my current business model. I made my systems more efficient, and I freed up even more time. With that extra time, I could focus on getting new business and making sure all parts of my business were getting adequate attention. It is funny how it works, but every time I hire someone new or add more hours to someone's work load, I find myself filling my newfound free time almost immediately. With the extra time, I can work on tasks I have been putting off or explore new streams of income. Knowing I have traded busy work for work that could produce new business and more money feels good.

There are 10 people on my team, including three people I have hired in the last year. Most days, I work from about 8:30 to 5:00, with time to play 9 holes of golf once or twice per week. I have the flexibility to go swimming with my family in the afternoon or to take the morning off if needed. I rarely work on the weekends; we usually go on two one-week vacations each year; and I go to a couple of conferences each year. I have learned not to drive myself into the ground but rather to hire someone to take more of that workload off me. I more than make up for the money I pay people through new work and opportunities that can create with that free time.

I have slowly built my team over time, adding a new person when I became too busy or saw an opportunity for increased income. I have buyer agents who work with buyers, and I receive a percentage of their commission for doing very little, if any, work. I have assistants who help with paperwork, reports, generating leads, communicating with title companies, marketing, and much more. In the past, I would work during most of my vacations, and it drove my wife crazy. Now I can go on vacation and not work at all!

When should you hire help?

Something I wish I would have realized well before I hired my first assistant is that doing everything myself is a huge mistake. The more work I had, the longer I worked, and the more I worked, the more fatigued I became. I have many different things going on at once, and that makes it fun yet stressful at times. I work on REOs, BPOS (broker price opinions), flips, regular sales, and other miscellaneous items. When I get really busy, I start making mistakes and forgetting work-related tasks. Mistakes in real estate can become very expensive. If I lose an REO client, it could cost me tens of thousands of dollars...or more! When I was busier, I was lucky to keep up with the important items, but with help, I can keep up so much better, and I actually have free time.

My advice to anyone running a business is to hire help before you think you need it. Even if you are handling things perfectly, ask yourself if you are you actually working on your business or working for your business? The reason we start our own business is to make more money, have more freedom, or both. A business owner's goals should include increasing profits, adding additional income streams, or starting new businesses. It is impossible for most business owners to accomplish these goals without help that handles the busy work. An assistant can take care of the busy work and will allow you to work on important, money-making activities. In my experience, the more free time I have, the more work that comes in. With free time, I can focus on new ideas and improving systems. Those new ideas almost always bring new opportunities and eventually more work and more money.

When people wait to hire help until they are too busy to handle all their current tasks, they run into a huge problem. They must find time to hire someone, train them, and make sure the new hire is doing their job correctly. How can someone possibly manage all those activities effectively if they don't have enough time to complete all the business tasks? The sooner you hire help, the easier the transition is and the less stress there is.

An assistant provides motivation!

Once you hire someone to help with your business, you become responsible for another person's income. This can be intimidating at first, but knowing you are helping someone take care of their family by providing them a job is very cool. Use this as motivation to improve your businesses. The better you do, and the more money you make, the more secure your assistant's job will be, and you may even be able to hire more people. The more successful you become, the more people you can hire. Plus, you help support your local economy.

An assistant helps provide new ideas

When you start your own business, you are immersed in the day-to-day activities, planning every aspect of that business. You eat, sleep, and dream about your business and how to make it succeed. When you are involved in something all the time, you may miss the simple things that can improve your business. We are so focused on making the business work perfectly that we miss obvious areas of improvement.

Hiring someone to help adds another mind to the mix. Even if the new assistant has no experience and no idea what your business is about, they'll still have a new perspective. Sometimes, that is exactly what you need to make your business work. A new hire can see simple areas of improvement that the owner may miss because they are so used to how things are done.

I would always encourage bosses to listen to their employees and promote an open-idea environment. The more ideas that are expressed, the better chance your team will discover great ideas. There is no rule that says a boss must implement every idea presented by an employee, so what do you have to lose?

Socializing can be a good thing for business owners

An assistant also gives you someone to socialize with. You have someone you can bounce ideas off of and talk to during the day. Many entrepreneurs start with just themselves, and the day can get boring. You can only talk to yourself or your desk for so long before you start to wonder if you are slowly losing it.

I would caution you about how much you socialize. You don't want to spend so much time talking that you don't get any work done. I see many people spend more time talking and gossiping than working. When you don't have a boss to keep you in line, you must make sure you keep yourself in line.

Training someone helps you train yourself

I've found that, while writing for my blog, I feel like I'm training a new worker. It has helped me dive deeper into real estate investing and learn new techniques. Writing also reinforces basic investing ideas and principles that I never thought about because I had been in real estate so long I thought I knew it all. When you train someone, you also train yourself. If you hire an assistant who has no idea what your business is about, you must teach them all the basics. I think this is a great way to remind yourself of the fundamentals of your business and look for ways to improve.

When you're training someone to do a new job, it is also a great time to put together a manual on how to perform the duties you require. You can even have the new hire put the manual together as they learn new tasks. If the new hire does not work out, or you need to hire more people in the future, the manual can make training new people much easier.

Vacations: time with your spouse and kids!

If you run your business as a one-man show, how can you take a vacation? If you can manage to take a vacation, you will probably be worrying the entire time about what could go wrong while you are away. An assistant may not be able to do as good a job as you, but they can handle most tasks and figure many things out on their own. At the very least, an assistant should be able to screen calls and only forward the really important issues that need to be dealt with immediately. Once you get an assistant or two who really know what they are doing, you can go on a work-free vacation! For many business owners, this is a dream that is too far away to seem possible.

Owning a business can also mean working long and crazy hours. Often, our families suffer because of the workload we take on. The sooner you can hire help and start delegating tasks, the more time and flexibility you will have. If an emergency comes up during your kid's soccer game and you don't have help, chances are you'll have to leave the game to take care of the problem. If you have an assistant, you have someone who can take care of the problem while you stay at the game to cheer on your child.

What do you hate doing in your business?

We all have tasks or things we must do in our business that drive us crazy. We procrastinate and hope they will magically do themselves while we sleep. The problem is those tasks never seem to go away on their own. If you hire help, you can delegate the tasks you dislike most to someone else. You can delegate accounting, expense tracking, answering the phone, filing reports, scheduling, and any other task you dislike. If your assistant does these tasks, not only do you have more free time, but you're also happier and enjoy your job more.

Time is money

I recently heard a great idea from Jack Canfield: delegate everything you do that's below your income level. So, if your time is worth $20 per hour and you can hire someone to do tasks for $10 per hour, do it! Time is our most valuable asset—we cannot buy more of it no matter how much money we have. Focus on the tasks that will make you more money and let someone else do the mundane one. Take the time to determine your hourly worth and which tasks you can hire out that are below your income level.

I recently started having someone else take care of my yard. In the past, I thought my duty as an American male was to mow the lawn, fertilize the grass, and pull weeds. I realized I can hire someone to do all of this, allowing me to spend more time with my family. Spending time with my family is much more important to me than to living up to a stereotype. I have started to analyze how I spend time in all aspects of my life and whether the things I am doing are worth the time they consume.

How to find a great assistant

I have been extremely lucky to hire good people whenever I need someone new. I think one of the reasons I have been lucky is I have used referrals from friends or co-workers. I always interview people and try to get a gut feeling for the person and if they will be a good worker or not. I also depend heavily on opinions from people I trust. I have hired people who did not interview well, but they were so well recommended that I hired them anyway. Those people have worked out great, and I could not be happier! My current assistant previously worked for my sister, but my sister could not give her enough hours. My sister gave a great recommendation, and the interview was basically done to go through the motions. A couple Realtors recommended another one of my assistants, and he has been great as well. If you are looking for help, I recommend asking everyone you know if they know someone who needs a job.

What if I can't afford an assistant?

If your budget is tight and you are worried you don't make enough money to hire help, there are other options. One great option I have never used but have heard many people rave about is hiring a virtual assistant. Virtual assistants can be hired from online companies and may be located in many different countries, including the United States. Virtual assistants can be extremely affordable, and you can customize your assistant to the tasks you need done. The more complex the job, the more expensive the assistant usually is. You can ask for an assistant who is a great writer, good with computers, can create a website, or does email marketing. The assistant can be full-time or work only a couple of hours per week.

Should you hire someone with experience or someone who is brand new to your business?

Many people want to hire someone with experience in their business field. They don't want to have to teach them everything because they don't have the time. Other people may want to hire someone with no experience whatsoever because they want a fresh slate to work with. I can go either way, as both points of view make sense. I advise interviewing someone thoroughly if they have experience in your field of work. The last thing you want is someone who thinks they know how to do everything but does it all wrong requires retraining. Retraining takes more time than training someone new because you must break old habits, and that can be very difficult.

Payroll, taxes, and reporting

Many people don't hire help because they don't want to bother with figuring out payroll, deducting taxes, and filing the necessary paperwork. There is a very simple solution to this problem: hire someone to take care of it for you. Many payroll companies will do everything necessary to pay that person, keep records, and file paperwork for you. I gave the job to one of my assistants and let them figure it all out with the help of my accountant.

If you want to make big money, work toward creating a team

Creating a real estate team can take time. You must first create a steady business that can support itself. Once you start getting busy, consider hiring help as soon as you can. If you hire a licensed agent or help them get licensed, they can sell houses as well and help pay for their own salary.

CHAPTER 31

How to Build a Real Estate Team

I've already advocated for building a team. As you know, ten people work on my team, and they help me complete tasks I don't like doing. They sell more houses and make my life easier by saving me time.

One of the hardest parts of being an agent or business owner is hiring people, but it must be done. Without help, you will always be on call, get stressed over the amount of work, go crazy over busy work, and be unhappy. The sooner you hire help, the better and easier your life will be, and you will make more money!

How does an agent know when they are ready to hire help?

Any agent should hire help as soon as they can afford it. The sooner you hire help, the more time you will have to train them, and the more time you will free up to pursue money-making activities. If you wait to hire help until you are busy enough to need it, how are you going to find time to train them? You need time to look for help, go through the screening process, and train.

When I was doing multiple BPOs and selling REOs, I worked long hours, and the busy work drove me crazy. Most of my time was spent taking care of paperwork and filling out reports, and I was ignoring prospecting for new business. I hired a general assistant to help with the busy work and any tasks that weren't vitally important. My assistant was not licensed and had no experience in real estate sales but had experience with property management. Hiring help made my life so much easier, and I immediately saw a huge jump in my production and sales.

My first assistant had some real estate experience but knew nothing about what I was doing with my real estate business. The drawback to someone with inexperience is you must teach them everything, but this is also a positive. If you must teach someone everything you know, you can teach them the right way to do things. If someone already has experience, they may have learned to do things the wrong way or different than how you want it done.

I think it is much easier to teach a new hire how to complete new tasks than to teach them how to do things they have done differently for years. We are creatures of habit, and breaking habits is hard. Training a new person may take more time and effort, but you will most likely experience fewer headaches in the future.

What should your new hire do?

The great thing about hiring someone to work for you is you are the boss. You can teach your assistant to do whatever you need help with. More than anything else, I needed help with BPOs, expense submissions, and paperwork. Those also happen to be the tasks I dislike doing the most, so hiring help improved my life.

Most agents don't do REO and BPO work, so the tasks you assign to your assistant may be much different. A traditional agent can use an assistant to help with contracts, marketing, web development, advertising, database maintenance, picture-taking, client communication, title company communication, and much more. Have your assistant do whatever you don't like doing (as long as it does not require a license...assuming they're unlicensed).

How will hiring help make you more money?

An agent must complete many tasks to be successful. If an agent does everything themselves, they probably aren't doing as good of a job as they could. There is not enough time in the day to market, contact your database, show houses, write contracts, create leads and set goals. When an agent hires help, they can teach the new person how to do tasks that are not being done or that are being done poorly. That leaves the agent more time to concentrate on tasks they like to do. It also leaves the agent more time to make sure everything is done well, and it leaves the agent time to set goals and plan their business. The more planning and goal setting an agent does, the more successful they will be. When an agent gets busy, they usually ignore goal setting and planning because it does not seem important. However, goal setting is one of the most important things any business owner can do!

You will have to pay someone to work for you, and it is tough for agents to give up their hard-earned money. The person you hire will allow you to make much more money than you will ever pay them because you will have more time to focus on what makes you money. When I hired help, I was able to focus on getting new REO clients and spend more time on my fix-and-flip business. I made much more money after hiring help than I did doing it all on my own.

How can agents continue to grow their team?

When an agent hires their first assistant, they usually see a big jump in production and wonder why they waited so long to hire someone! With more time and more help, they can do more deals and make more money. With that growth comes more listings, and more listings create more leads. When you start generating enough leads, you can hire another agent.

How to add a new agent to your team

Hiring another agent to join your team is a little trickier than hiring an assistant. First, you must know how your broker handles teams and commission splits. Then, you must decide how to pay your new agent. Many books and coaches suggest a 50/50 split for newer agents, with the team leader paying the agent's expenses. More-experienced agents may not join your team for a 50/50 split, and you may have to pay them a 70/30 split or come up with another arrangement. Some teams will give agents different splits depending on if the agent received the lead from the team or on their own.

Should you hire an experienced agent?

I have hired both new and experienced agents with varying degrees of success. New agents can be very motivated, will work for a smaller commission split, and can be trained easily. However, new agents need more training and guidance and may not sell as many houses as an experienced agent.

More-experienced agents will want a higher commission split and less training but will sell more houses (hopefully). If you are training your agents to use a system, more-experienced agents may be harder to train. I prefer newer agents because I can train them to use systems that will make them successful, and they will listen to me! Getting a new agent to sell multiple houses and generate income for you may take more time, but when they do start selling houses, they will make you much more money than an experienced agent.

Why would an agent join your team?

Agents have no boss telling them what to do. They must make themselves work hard and do the things they need to do to make money. Some agents are self-driven and do very well while others don't. Teams can provide agents with a structure that allows them to succeed. Your assistant can help your agents with paperwork and other tasks. You can also pay some of your agents' costs, like MLS fees, board dues, or office fees. If your agents are selling houses, the money you make from their sales will more than make up for these costs.

I have ten plus people on my team. I say "plus" because I have both part-time help and people who help out on occasion but do put in many hours. Four of my agents work on both leads we provide and their own clients. I have one full-time licensed assistant and one full-time unlicensed assistant. I also have a licensed team manager who sells houses. I have a part-time bookkeeper who helps with paperwork and random tasks. I have three people who take pictures and do inspections in various locations, but they only work a couple of hours per week. We are hiring a new agent very soon. I help run the team with my manager. I sell my own listings, work with occasional buyers, run the fix-and-flip business, and write a blog. Various team members also help with the fix-and-flips and property management for my rental properties.

I have a lot going on, and there is no way I could handle it all without a great team. People may think a big team makes things more complicated, but it makes everything easier. I can go on vacation without working; I can focus on money-making activities or the things I like doing; and I can let my team handle other tasks. I don't mess with payroll because I hired my manager to figure all of that out. Teams help you do everything better and provide better service to your clients.

CHAPTER 32

How Real Estate Conferences Improve Business

Real estate conferences are a great source of information, inspiration, and ways to improve business. During the year, I attend many conferences specific to my line of work, and I suggest you do as well. Unless you're an REO agent, I wouldn't attend REO conferences, but there are many local and national conferences for traditional agents. Conferences not only give you a chance to learn, but they also offer many other benefits. You will meet other agents while taking time off from the daily grind, which may be more valuable than anything you learn.

I have attended the National REO Brokers Association (NRBA) annual conference since 2009. The NRBA is a great organization that helps REO agents with their business, systems, referrals, and anything else an REO agent could possibly need. The conference doesn't entail just classroom activities. It includes a golf tournament, poker night, and many other fun things.

There are conferences for every type of business, and you do not have to be an REO agent to take advantage of them. There are conferences for traditional agents, short sale agents, relocation agents, and new constructions agents.

Conferences allow you to network with like-minded people

The main goal of a conference is to provide information that helps my business, and it allows me to meet clients in person. However, I usually get more out of a conference by networking with other agents. At one conference, I met five agents who were also investing in real estate, either by flipping or holding long-term rentals. Not only had I talked with many agents about the REO industry, but I also had a chance to pick their brains about their investing strategies. Just because this was an REO conference, it didn't mean I couldn't learn about any number of subjects. This conference offered a huge amount of information on topics that helped grow an agent's wealth by other means than listing REO properties. Talking with other agents definitely improves business.

Conferences give me a chance to think differently

During a normal work week, I am busy completing tasks, inspecting properties, or doing other work-related items. At conferences, I am in a completely different state of mind. During conferences, I focus on how I can improve my business. I think many of us get caught up in day-to-day routines and forget about the big picture and where we want to end up. A conference forces you to think about that big picture and think about new ideas and techniques that can ultimately make you more money. At this particular conference, there were many speakers and panels that focused on how agents can make more money and add new income streams.

Conferences force you to delegate

When I attend a conference, I don't have the time to focus on my daily tasks. I must rely on my staff to get everything done correctly. Allowing your staff to complete tasks is extremely scary when you first do it. It is a big step, but to get to where we all want to be, it is a necessary step. To list houses, complete BPOs, do my inspections, flip houses, invest in houses, and write my blog, I must have help. There simply is not enough time in the day for me to do it all plus spend time with my family.

When I attend conferences or go on vacation, I'm forced to delegate to my staff. Most successful business owners know a business should be able to run without the owner and still make money. Many of us have a really hard time delegating anything to anyone because we think it will be done incorrectly. If you want the time and success we all want, you must be able to let go and let your staff take care of things.

Conferences offer the chance to make lifelong friends

I meet so many agents and clients at conferences that it is hard to keep track of them all. With each person I meet, I can pick their brain on investing, REO, and what they like to do in their personal life. Meeting new people and finding lifelong friends is a great experience. I have received many referrals and learned great business ideas from people I have met at conferences. Many people attend conferences for the scheduled events, but often, you can learn more from other attendees rather than the speakers. I keep in touch with many of my conference friends though email or Facebook.

Conferences provide new business ideas

At almost every conference I attend, I learn something new. I learn about a new way to make money or a better way to run my business. I cannot implement everything I learn, and changing my entire business based on one conference doesn't make sense. However, if I can implement one thing that improves my business, the conference was beneficial. It does not even have to be related to the conference goals. I love talking to as many people as I can and learning what is going on in their business and lives.

Conferences provide fundamentals

No matter how long we have been working at a job or have been in a field of business, we forget the fundamentals. Fundamentals are what made us successful, and conferences remind us of everything we need to do to be successful. I am reminded of how important it is to communicate with my clients frequently and keep them updated on their properties. Often, we forget the basics because we are too concerned with exploring new business.

How do you get the most out of a business conference?

I have attended some bad conferences. I have had to sit through horrible material with very few people in attendance. However, I still get something out of bad conferences. You must bring a great attitude and expect to learn a ton. If you think the conference will be a horrible failure and you won't learn anything, you probably won't. Even conferences that are giant sales funnels and teach you nothing can be beneficial. Here are some tips to get the most out of a conference:

- **Talk to everyone:** I don't care if you are shy—get over it. I was shy when I was younger, and getting over it was one of the best things I did, both professionally and personally. Most conference attendees are not comfortable because they are in a different environment. The more people you talk to, the more friends you will make and the more comfortable you will get. If someone doesn't like you, who cares, as you will probably never see them again.

- **Talk to different people:** If you make some friends at a conference, try not to hang out with them all the time. It's fine to mingle and spend time with them, but sit with different people at lunch. You should also sit in different spots at the conference. Meet as many new people as you can.

- **Show up to the sessions:** Many people pay for a conference, look at the agenda, and then decide they don't need to go to half of the sessions. Attend every session you can because you never know what you will learn. Some of my best ideas come from subjects that I already know a lot about or have no interest in. If you don't show up, you have no chance of learning.

- **Bring plenty of business cards:** I usually hand out at least 50 business cards at conferences. You never know who you will meet who can help you. If you receive business cards, write a note on the back detailing who the person is and how you met them. You'll meet a lot of people and will easily forget names.

- **Take notes**: When you attend sessions, take a lot of notes. Forgetting things is really easy, and no matter how much you think you will remember, you won't. Write down everything that is interesting to you.
- **Don't be that guy:** At one conference I attended, there was a party and open bar on the last night. Many people went crazy and made a fool of themselves. I see no problem with having a good time, but don't get to the point where you are slurring your words and can't walk straight amongst people who may want to do business with you.

What do you do after the conference?

Attending the conference is just part of the process. When you get home, you also have work to do. Many people attend a conference, take pages of notes, get back home, and forget about it all. They are too tired or busy with work to look at the notes. One of the first things you should do when you get home is review your notes and the people you met. Prioritize the things and people who can make the biggest difference in your life, and create tasks for yourself. This can involve writing thank you cards, following up on emails or calls, researching new ideas, etc. You must make a list, and you must review everything right away or you won't do it.

What did I gain from the conference I attended?

Here is a short list of things I learned or gained from my conference:

- **At least five new contacts:** These were solid contacts who could make me more money, not just people I spoke with.
- **Solidified connections with people I already knew:** If you attend the same type of conference over and over, you will see the same people and make friends. When people repeatedly see you at events, they'll know you are serious about the business. This is extremely important for REO agents.

- **Was forced to let my business run by itself:** I have worked very hard on my real estate team, rentals, flips and the blog. I did almost no work while attending the conference. I only called my wife and kids, and things went extremely smoothly. Most of my business can run very well by itself. The blog takes a lot of personal work since I write everything myself, but it is a lot of fun for me, and taking a few days or a week off from writing is not the end of the world.
- **Met some famous people:** At most conferences, there will be someone famous to attract guests. I have seen George W. Bush speak, taken a picture with Spud Webb, and talked to many other notable people.

If you want to be a successful agent, I highly suggest attending conferences

I encourage everyone to attend conferences for their work or for investing. Conferences help my business, create relationships, and make me more successful. The NRBA conference is restricted to members, and it is not easy to get into even if you are an experienced REO agent. This conference is not a possibility for most people, but there are tons of conferences all over the country for every industry. Conferences are a great way for anyone to increase their productivity, better their business, and network. Conferences improve business; I learn this over and over every time I attend one.

CHAPTER 33

Investing in Real Estate While Working as an Agent

I am an avid real estate investor and write about both being an agent and investing on my blog at InvestFourMore.com. For people who want to invest in real estate, becoming an agent makes perfect sense. Being an agent saves you a ton of money and gets you more deals. Being a Realtor has helped me with my own investing strategy tremendously. I have purchased 16 long-term rental properties and over 100 flips in the last ten years. Because I am a Realtor, I save thousands on each transaction.

If you plan to buy more than one or two rental properties each year, get your real estate license! If you do nothing else with your license except buy your own rental properties, it will save you thousands in commissions every year. On every rental property I buy, I save a ton of money because I get paid a commission as the buyer's agent. It may be 2%, 2.5%, or 3% per deal, but in the end, that adds up to a lot of money. If you buy three houses per year and are an agent, you can save $7,500 to $9,000 if the average price is $100,000.

If you are already an agent, I want you to consider investing in real estate. Real estate is an incredible investment and is much better than the stock market. An agent has a huge advantage when it comes to investing in rental properties or fix and flips, as you will soon learn.

Advantages of being an investor with a real estate license

There are many other advantages to being an investor with a real estate license. It saves commissions and allows me to get more deals. Here are some more reasons having a license is a huge advantage:

- As an agent, you get access to the MLS and can do your own property searches without relying on an agent to find you the right deal. Having access to MLS gives investors a tremendous advantage because they don't have to wait for an agent to send them listings. I search for listings at least five times per day, and I routinely make offers the same day a house is listed. An agent can also easily pull sold comparable information from the MLS to calculate values on properties. Calculating accurate values is one of the most important things an investor needs to do to be successful.

- As an agent, you can fraternize with other agents and people in the real estate business. The more people you know in the business, the more people you can tell that you are looking for property. Sometimes the best deals are those that are brought to you, not those you find yourself. Let everyone you know you are looking for investment properties, and you never know what will come up.

- The IRS puts limits on how much money you can deduct on rental properties if real estate is not your primary job. If real estate is your primary job, you may be able to deduct many more expenses.

- If you are an agent, chances are other agents will know who you are and know if you are dependable. If you have a good reputation, you may be able to get a deal based on the fact that other agents know you are serious and will deliver.

Because I am an agent, I save 2 to 6 percent on every property I buy and sell. As a result, I can buy investment property for more than the average investor. We complete about 10 to 15 flips per year, and in order to buy that many houses, we have to make very competitive offers. There is a lot of investor competition in our area, and any advantage we can get makes a huge difference. When I know I am going to save 6 percent on each deal, I can offer 6 percent more than an investor without their license can. This is a huge advantage and gets me many more deals than I would get if I was not an agent.

I have a pretty sweet deal with my broker, and I get a 100 percent commission split after I pay a flat fee to my broker every year. Many agents will have to pay more money to their broker if they have a different split, but they will still save a lot of money on their own deals.

CHAPTER 34

The Top Reason Real Estate Agents Fail

Many agents have a very hard time getting started in the business. As you know, an agent's average income is less than $40,000 because so many agents fail to make much money. Agents don't make much money for many reasons .

If you want to become or already are an agent, you need to avoid these mistakes to make sure you are successful. Agents can get distracted, frustrated, or lose focus easily. Success never comes easy, but real estate is a business with unlimited potential if you are willing to work at it.

Why do real estate agents make less than $40,000 per year?

The average-income figure can be very deceiving. If you simply look at the averages, real estate looks like a horrible business endeavor. Agents don't make much money, have no benefits, and have no retirement plan. However, as a successful agent, I think I have a much better retirement plan than most people: rental properties.

What are the top ten mistakes agents make?

1. Not saving enough money to live on before becoming an agent. When you become an agent, you are basically starting a business. Because building your business will take time, you can't expect to quit your job and start selling houses your first month first. Making your first sale can take months. One of my agents ran out of money before he sold his first house. He quit and moved to another job because he had a family to support.

2. Trying to become a successful agent while working a full-time job. One of the hardest things to do is begin a real estate career working only part time. People want to view houses, talk to their agent, and receive information quickly. If a buyer can only reach you after 5 or on the weekends, they will become very frustrated and have a hard time finding a house in a seller's market. As a part-time agent, you won't have time to market yourself, hold open houses, make calls, and do the other activities that bring you business.

3. Chase shiny objects. When you become an agent, many companies will try to sell you leads or the front page of Google ad space. The salesman is very convincing, and they will probably convince you that paying them is a good business decision because "just one commission will pay for their service." While some companies do provide worthwhile leads, most don't. The quality of leads from the internet is usually low, and you will be much better off if you make calls or in-person visits yourself. Many agents blow through their marketing budget by signing up for every online lead service they can.

4. Ignoring or failing to return phone calls. An agent's business is based on relationships. It is based on talking to people, building trust, and selling houses. If you do a good job, those you sell houses to or for will recommend you to their friends and family. Many agents spend a lot of money trying to get people to call or email them. You'd be amazed how many agents don't answer their phone or return calls! I have personally left messages and sent emails to many agents looking to refer business or even buy houses myself in other states, and most never call back. I don't care how bad a lead sounds when they leave a message—call them back. You never know who their friends are or how able to buy or sell they are until you talk to them.

5. Fail to market to their database. An agent's database may be the most valuable thing they have. All agents should keep a database of past clients, potential clients, business contacts, and anyone else they know. You can send your contacts letters, emails, and invite them to fun events. A good database will make the top agents the most money, and many agents are too lazy to create one. Most agents who have a database are then too lazy to actually use it (initially, I was one of those agents who did not keep a good database, and I struggled for it).

6. Choose the wrong broker. New agents need training. The more training you get, the more successful you will be. However, many new agents choose the broker who has the lowest fees and highest commission split to the agent. If you are a new agent and do not know how to sell houses, pick the broker with the best training program. Is it better to sell 20 houses your first year and keep 50 percent of the commissions or sell one house your first year and keep 100 percent of the commission?

7. Start working for a property management company. I think it is great if a new agent can find a team to work with in the beginning. They may even get paid hourly to work as an assistant. However, many agents ask me if it is smart to start off working with a property management company. Property managers manage rentals; for the most part, they do not sell houses. If you want to learn how to sell houses, do not work for a property manager.

8. Don't set goals or make a plan. When I started, I did not set goals, and I struggled for a long time. I also did not make a business plan or any house-selling plan. Then, I started setting goals and making plans, and my business boomed. I went from selling 15 houses per year to over 100 houses within a couple of years. REO played a large role in that, but I would have never found REO if I had not set goals and planned my business. As an agent, you won't have a boss to tell you what to do. You must make your own plan and motivate yourself.

9. Sacrifice their clients' needs for a commission check. Many agents find themselves in a position where a deal is falling apart. Maybe the buyer's inspection found a major issue, the appraisal came in low, or the buyer's loan was more expensive than they thought. Will you be the agent that does what is best for their client or the agent that does whatever it takes to get a commission check? Real estate is about relationships and referrals. If you do what is best for yourself, word gets around, and fewer people will use you. If you do what is best for your clients, word gets around, and more clients will come your way.

10. Do not plan for the expenses that come with being an agent. Agents are self-employed. They have no real boss and no employer who deducts taxes. You must plan for taxes, health insurance, and retirement. If you want a corporate job with benefits and a set salary, being an is not for you. You also must plan for retirement, but I think being an agent has retirement advantages.

Being an agent is not a walk in the park, and the money doesn't come easily. If you treat is as a business and plan accordingly, you can be very successful. You won't have a boss, you can plan your own schedule, and you'll realize investing advantages. If you take shortcuts, go for the easy money, and fail to work hard, you will struggle.

CHAPTER 35

How to Make One Million Dollars per Year as a Real Estate Agent

Making one million dollars within one year seems like an impossible goal for many people. Real estate is great in that you can make money in multiple ways, and there is no ceiling to how much you can make. As you know, I run my own real estate business. The amount of money I make depends on how well I plan, the goals I set, and the work ethic I possess.

The median annual income for a full-time Realtor is $54,000, but many agents make much more than that. My team sold over 200 houses in 2014, which brought in over $650,000 in real estate commissions from almost $25 million in sales volume. I did not make $650,000 because I had to pay commissions, expenses, and our staff. However, many agents all over the United States make at least one million dollars within a year. The best part is you neither need a college or even a high school education (depending on the state). However, you do have to work hard, plan well, and network effectively.

How much money do the best agents make?

I think $650,000 in gross commissions and 25 million in sales volume was pretty good, but it is not even close to what the top agents in the country make. According to Realtrends.com, in 2013, the top agent in the country had over $668 million in sales volume, and the agent ranked 250th had over $60 million in sales volume. Note that Realtrends.com does not include all the top agents in their figures. They only count agents that apply with Realtrends.com or that they find through their own searches. Many top agents who do not apply or are missed are left off the list, and some agents ask to be excluded.

The top agents in the country are not the only ones who make a lot of money. My office has 45 agents, and most of them work part time. Still, three of our agents made over $300,000 last year.

How does sales volume translate to income?

Sales volume is the total of the sales price of all houses an agent sells. It's not the money an agent earns. On my REO listings, I get paid between 1 percent and 3 percent for each sale, and my average commission is about 2.7% of the sales price. Remember, there is no typical or standard sales commission, and all commissions are negotiable. If we apply these numbers to the agent ranked 250th in the country, we can assume income of $1.6 million from $60 million in sales volume. There is a good chance a retail agent who doesn't specialize in REO listings earns more than a 2.7 percent commission on each deal, but we'll use 2.7 percent to stay conservative.

The top agent in the country may earn over $18 million in commissions from $680 million in sales volume. To sell that many houses, that agent must have a large staff, and he will need to pay his agents out of that $18 million.

Does an agent with $60 million in sales volume net more than $1 million?

Even though an with $60 million in sales volume will most likely earn $1.6 million in commissions, they don't get to keep it all. Agents must pay all their costs and may have to pay a split to their broker if they do not own their own office.

An agent that sells multiple houses also needs help. Unless your average sale is $1 million or more, completing enough transactions to reach that figure requires help. I have two full-time assistants, and I don't come close to that much sales volume, but I also have a relatively low median price. An agent will have to pay for marketing costs, MLS fees, staff, office fees, licensing fees, and more. If you run a real estate team, you also won't keep 100% of the commissions because you must pay commissions to agents on your team who are actually selling houses and doing the work.

A general rule of thumb is an agent needs sales volume of $50 million to net $1 million per year. Net profit is the amount left over after all expenses are paid. Going by that math, at least 250 real estate agents in the country make at least $1 million per year. However, when we consider some other factors, many more agents may net that much.

How many real estate agents earn $1 million per year?

It This is hard to determine because Realtrends.com does not include every agent on their list. Plus, every agent's expenses and team structure is different. Some agents may need $1.5 million in commissions to net $1 million, and others may only need $1.2 million. Also, the Realtrends.com list only includes individual agents. They also provide a list that includes teams. That list includes 250 teams with over $60 million in sales volume.

Even though agents on a team split commissions, I would bet 95% of team leaders still earn over $1 million after expenses. That means at least 500 agents make over $1 million per year in the United States.

How many houses does an agent need to sell to earn $1 million per year?

To reach this figure, you must sell many houses. However, sales prices can affect that number. The number of houses you must sell will depend on how expensive the houses are. If the average sales price is $1 million, you must only sell 50 to hit the $1 million mark. Most agents don't work in areas that will allow them to sell 50 $1 million houses within a year. If you combine sales numbers from all agents in my area, you won't find 50 $1 million houses being sold in a year.

Where I work, the average sales price is around $200,000, which means I would have to sell 250 houses to reach $50 million in sales volume. However, since I sell REOs, my sales price is lower than the median sales price. I would have to sell over 300 houses to net $1 million in annual income. That is a tough number to reach, but it is possible, and it's one of my goals! In 2013, the top team in the country (run by John Murray), sold over 1,200 houses!

For an agent with a median sale price of $400,000, $1 million in annual income becomes much more realistic. That agent needs only sell 125 houses to reach $1 million in net income. That's still a tough number to reach, but it is possible. You would have to sell just over 10 houses per month and two to three per week. Getting to that volume requires building relationships, generating leads, and taking care of your clients, all of which take time. If you do all of those things, selling that many houses is possible.

How likely is $1 million in net annual income?

Reaching $1 million in net annual income takes a lot of work, planning, and some luck. Most agents won't even earn $100,000, as the median income for a full-time Realtor is $54,000. As we discussed earlier, most agents aren't very good. They don't take care of their clients, follow up with leads, or plan their business. If you use systems, train your team. and set goals, $1 million in income is attainable. Most agents will never come close to that, but remember, most agents work part-time and don't treat being an agent as a business. I can almost guarantee that you won't make $1 million annually in the corporate world unless you become a CEO or get lucky with stock options. The length of time it takes to become a CEO or the path you must take in order to get there is more likely to be determined by politics as opposed to hard work. Real estate lets you create your own path to success, with no one else to answer to.

Agents don't just make money from selling houses

Agents can do more than sell houses. I flip 10-15 houses per year, and I also own 16 rental properties. I hope to make over $1 million per year very soon by using a mix of house sales, flips, income from rental properties, and income from BPOs and my blog. Even if you never get to a point where you make $1 million annually just from selling houses, being an agent opens doors that will allow you to add income streams and make more money in other businesses.

Why I love being an agent

One reason being an agent is better than working in the corporate world is there is no ceiling. There is no limit to the amount of money you can make, either as an agent, investor, or business owner. In the corporate world, reaching $1 million in income will be tough unless you start your own corporation or become a CEO. It takes years of 80-hour weeks to reach CEO, and that's something I never want to do (I don't even want to work 80 hours in one week, let alone every week). Plus, there is no guarantee you will make CEO or even keep your corporate job.

There is no guarantee you will make $1 million annually in real estate either. But I think you have a better chance of becoming wealthy by creating your own business as opposed to working for someone else. I truly believe becoming an agent is one of the best ways to start your own business.

Get Started Creating Your Future!

I hope this book has provided you with the information you need to succeed as a real estate agent. At the very least, I hope it's made you think about whether you want to be an agent or not. I love real estate and the life it has provided me, and I think almost anyone can succeed in real estate if they work at it and have a plan. If you want to be an agent, start writing out your goals, your plans, your marketing ideas, and when you want to accomplish them. If you have questions for me or want to learn more about investing in real estate, please visit InvestFourMore.com or email me at mailto:mark@investfourmore.com.

What Is the Next Step?

When I coach people, my goal is to **help them make as much money in real estate as they possibly can.** Different people have different goals and like doing different things. I help some investors buy more rentals; I help others learn to flip; and I even help people become successful agents. Two of the agents on my team made over $100,000 in their first year! Not everyone will realize results like those, but there is a lot of money to be made in real estate.

I found success in real estate, and that is my focus. If you want to get involved in real estate, I would love to help you learn the ins and outs. It is not as easy as they make it look on television.

If you invest the right way, rental properties and flips can change your life. They changed my life by giving me a better way to invest, a better way to make money, and a better way to retire. I am 37 years old and am in a better position to retire right now than most people will ever be. I am by no means done! Being an agent was vital to my investing because I made a lot of money as an agent, and it is easier to invest if you have a real estate license.

Don't forget to check out everything that's happening on my blog. I have a podcast, a forum, the blog, eBooks, paperback books, coaching programs, and many videos. I encourage you to sign up for my email list if you have not already done so. The emails I send you will help you navigate through the site, give you the most valuable resources, and help you decide how much or little you want to be involved with real estate.

- If you are interested in becoming an agent, sign up here: https://investfourmore.com/real-estate-agent-email-subscription/
- If you are interested in investing as well, sign up here: https://investfourmore.com/real-estate-investor-email-subscription/
- If you want to learn even more about rentals, I recently wrote Build a Rental Property Empire, which is available as an eBook or paperback and checks in at

over 350 pages of valuable info. This book is a best-seller and an incredible resource.
https://www.amazon.com/Build-Rental-Property-Empire-no-nonsense/dp/1530663946/ref=as_li_ss_tl?ie=UTF8&psc=1&refRID=3QPDHQK3AB4JAKYBBP9Y&linkCode=ll1&tag=inve05-20&linkId=df2ab4ac1150e25310f3313db5969339

- If you are interested in flipping houses, I wrote a full-length book on how I have flipped over 100 houses and average over $30,000 from each. It's called Fix and Flip Your Way to Financial Freedom:
https://www.amazon.com/Fix-Flip-Your-Financial-Freedom/dp/1517318084/ref=as_li_ss_tl?ie=UTF8&dpID=51kysLjco1L&dpSrc=sims&preST=_AC_UL320_S R214,320_&psc=1&refRID=3QPDHQK3AB4JAKYBBP 9Y&linkCode=ll1&tag=inve05-20&linkId=462bb326fcc11fc35cc4f60cc21bd783

- I also wrote a book on success (How to Change Your Mindset to Achieve Huge Success). It covers how changing your outlook on life as well as your habits can make you rich. Attitude and mindset has so much to do with how happy and successful we are.
https://www.amazon.com/Change-Your-Mindset-Achieve-Success/dp/1535004479/ref=as_li_ss_tl?ie=UTF8&dpID=51xco7xY+ZL&dpSrc=sims&preST=_AC_UL320_ SR214,320_&psc=1&refRID=B4G2QH8BXA1EW47PR QXE&linkCode=ll1&tag=inve05-20&linkId=5b7982a841dd307b02d4e72b96039a7e

I have made my books and coaching products as affordable as possible. I know people who are starting out in a new business do not have a lot of extra money. For those of you who know you need a little extra push and accountability, I created more in-depth training courses. These come with conference calls and email training with me personally. The Six Figure Real Estate Agent Success System is a program I created that comes with personal coaching from me as well as audio CDs/MP3s, videos, a huge how-to guide, and much more. If you are interested, send me an email, and I may have a special coupon for those that read this book all the way through! Mark@investfourmore.com.

I hope you enjoyed the book, and if you want to connect with me on social media, check out the links below:

- Facebook
- LinkedIn
- Twitter
- Instagram
- Google +

About Mark Ferguson

I created Invest Four More to help people become real estate investors, either as rental property owners, flippers, wholesalers, agents, and even note owners. You may see pictures of me with my Lamborghini. It is a 1999 Diablo, which I bought in 2014. I had dreamed of owning a Lamborghini since I was a kid, and one of my publicly stated goals was buying one by 2014. Reaching that goal was an awesome experience. My readers helped hold me accountable to it. I even make sure I buy my cars below market value. I bought this car for $126,000, and two years later, it is worth about double that.

The car is not a flashy marketing ploy but a reward for hard work and a reminder that we really can have what we want if we put our mind to it.

How did I get started?

I have been a licensed Realtor since 2001. My father has been a Realtor since 1978, and in my youth, I was surrounded by real estate. When I was three, I remember sleeping under my dad's desk while he worked tirelessly in the office. Surprisingly (or perhaps not) I never wanted anything to do with real estate. In 2001, I graduated from the University of Colorado with a degree in business finance. I could not find a job that was appealing to me, so I reluctantly decided to work with my father part-time. Fifteen years later, I am sure glad I got into the real estate business!

Even though I had help getting started, I did not find success until five years into the business. I tried to follow my father's path, which did not mesh well with me. I found my own path as an REO agent, and my career took off. Many people think working with my father gave me a huge advantage, and he was a great help, but I think I actually would have been more successful sooner if I had been working on my own, forced to find my own path.

Now, I run a real estate team of 10. My team sells 100 to 200 houses each year. I flip 10-15 houses per year, and I own 16 long-term rentals. I love real estate and investing because of the money I can make and the freedom running my own business brings. I also love big goals, and one of those goals is my plan to purchase 100 rental properties by January 2023.

I started Invest Four More in March 2013, and the primary objective was to provide information on investing in long-term rentals. I was not a writer at any time in my life until I started my blog. In fact, since college, I had not written anything besides a basic letter. Readers who have been with me from the beginning may remember how tough it was to read my first articles, which were full of typos and poor grammar (I know—it is still not perfect!). My goal has always been to provide incredible information, not to provide perfect articles with perfect grammar.

The name "InvestFourMore" is a play on words indicating that it is possible to finance more than four properties. The blog provides articles on financing, finding, buying, rehabbing, and renting rental properties. The blog also discusses mortgage paydown strategies, flips, advice for agents, and many other real estate related topics.

I live in Greeley Colorado, which is about 50 miles north of Denver. I married my beautiful wife, Jeni, in 2008 and we have twins who turned five in June of 2016. When we met in 2005, Jeni was a Realtor but has since put her license on ice while she takes care of the twins. Jeni loves to sew and makes children's dresses under the label Kaiya Papaya.

Outside of work, I love to travel, play golf, and work/play with <u>my cars.</u>

Acknowledgements

I could not be where I am at without a lot of help from many people. When I first started in real estate, I tried to go at it alone. I thought I was smart and could figure it out, without anyone else telling me how to do things. I let my ego make some very bad decisions for me. Here are a few people I have to thank:

My Dad Jim Ferguson, who has been an entrepreneur most of his life. He taught me a lot about flipping houses and being a real estate agent. He was very patient with me when I was not patient with myself.

My wife Jeni, who has been incredibly supportive through the good times and the bad. The year I met her (2006), I made $28,000. In the beginning, things were not easy, and it was a struggle for me to break out of the grind and find my way in real estate. She was there for me when I started to find success and was working 80 or more hours per week to get everything done. She put up with me working during vacations and never really taking time off in the beginning. Luckily, I was able to create a business where we can now take real vacations without me working. I rarely work more than 40 hours per week (if that), and we have a wonderful family. Most importantly, she supported my car addiction!

Justin Gesso is my team manager and keeps our team together. He works with our agents, helps with the blog, helps with my coaching programs, helps with my books, and keeps me sane. Thank you, Justin!

Nikki True has been my assistant for 6 years. She was the person who helped me stop working 80 hours per week and take control of my life. She has always been extremely proactive, has an incredible work ethic, and has been willing to work on any project. She is now helping me with my flipping business and is doing an amazing job.

John Pfalzgraff has been our team's contract manager for many years. He is the reason I can make offers while I am still viewing a house. He keeps tabs on all the details that I hate thinking about. He is integral to both our agents' success and mine.

Jack Canfield's coaching was a program I took a few years ago. It gave me the confidence to buy my father's business, take the blog to new levels, hire more staff, and take more chances. Not only that, but I gained more freedom, reduced my stress, and am a happier person because of it. I still talk to personal coach John Beaman on a monthly basis.

Josh Elledge with Upend PR has helped me be featured on numerous major media sites like Washington Post, Yahoo, Zillow, The Street, Forbes, and many more.

Made in the USA
San Bernardino, CA
28 September 2017